BORING

— TO —

BRAVO

BORING
— TO —
BRAVO

PROVEN PRESENTATION TECHNIQUES
to ENGAGE, INVOLVE, *and* INSPIRE
YOUR AUDIENCE *to* ACTION

KRISTIN ARNOLD

GREENLEAF
BOOK GROUP PRESS

Published by Greenleaf Book Group Press
Austin, Texas
www.gbgpress.com

Distributed by Greenleaf Book Group LLC

For ordering information or special discounts for bulk purchases, please contact Greenleaf Book Group LLC at PO Box 91869, Austin, TX 78709, 512.891.6100.

Design and composition by Greenleaf Book Group LLC
Cover design by Greenleaf Book Group LLC
Illustrations by Shannon Parish, www.ShannonParish.com

Publisher's Cataloging-In-Publication Data
(Prepared by The Donohue Group, Inc.)

Arnold, Kristin J.

    Boring to bravo : proven presentation techniques to engage, involve, and inspire your audience to action / Kristin Arnold. -- 1st ed.

    p. ; cm.

    Includes bibliographical references.

    ISBN: 978-1-60832-036-3

    1. Public speaking--Handbooks, manuals, etc. 2. Business presentations--Handbooks, manuals, etc. I. Title.

PN4129.15 .A76 2010

808.5/1   2010927679

ISBN 13: 978-1-60832-036-3

Part of the Tree Neutral™ program, which offsets the number of trees consumed in the production and printing of this book by taking proactive steps, such as planting trees in direct proportion to the number of trees used: www.treeneutral.com

Printed in the United States of America on acid-free paper

10 11 12 13 14 15   10 9 8 7 6 5 4 3 2 1

First Edition

CONTENTS

Foreword ix

Preface xi

Introduction 1

CHAPTER 1   Have an Engaging Mind-set 11

It's About Them, Not About You • Be Passionate • Be Yourself • Have a Conversation • Collaborate with Them • Prepare for Inevitable Resistance

CHAPTER 2   Set an Interactive Tone 23

Reach Out and Connect with Your Audience • Grab 'Em with a Lively Title • Build on the Meeting Theme • Make the Room More Engaging • Prepare Your Handouts, Workbooks, or Takeaways • Pack Everything You Need • Observe and Mingle • Engage as They Enter • Start Smartly

CHAPTER 3   You Are the Number One Visual 43

Connect with Your Eyes • Smiles and other Facial Expressions • Spice it Up with Vocal Variety • Use Inviting Gestures • Move with a Purpose • Dress the Part

CHAPTER 4   Engage with Enhancing Visuals 57

Some General Principles • Use Props • Reward Your Audience • Be Spontaneous with an Easel Chart

CHAPTER 5   Use PowerPoint with Purpose 65

Use a Splash Page, Icons, and Hyperlinks • Insert Digital Pictures • Insert Cartoons, Symbols, and Drawings • Use Display Charts • Insert Video Snippets • Use Color Appropriately • Countdown Timers • Make Sure Your Slides Are Easy on the Eyes

CHAPTER 6 Ask Engaging Questions 81

Ask an Open-Ended Question • Ask a Situational Question • Ask a Provocative Question • Ask a Rhetorical Question • Take a Poll • Using Technology • Ask a Series of "Enrolling" Questions • Encourage Answers from the Audience • Interview a Participant • Wrong Answers and Other Maladies

CHAPTER 7 Q&A 99

Take Questions as You Go • Stop Periodically • Create Small Groups • Starting Your Q&A Session • Collect Questions • Respond to a Question • Answer the Question • Finish with a Strong Closing

CHAPTER 8 Let Your Natural Humor Shine Through 111

A Word About Finding Your Humor Comfort Zone • Making Humor Work for You • Finding the Common Ground • Keep Your Humor Eyes Open • Other Sources of Humor • The Pure Humor of Spontaneous Interaction • What About Jokes? •

CHAPTER 9 Choose Descriptive Words 125

Anchor Your Main Idea • Repetition, Restatement, and the Rule of Three • Use Strong Words • Choose Vivid Words • Arrange Words Rythmically to Resonate with Your Audience • The Power of the Pause • Lists, Headlines, and Highlights • Use Words that Sell • Keep it Simple

CHAPTER 10 Tell Interesting Stories 139

Definitions, Quotations, and Testimonials • Examples, Illustrations, and Case Studies • Comparisons, Analogies, and Allusions • Facts and Statistics • Personal and Signature Stories • Borrowed Stories • Invite Them into Your Story • Autoresponders

CHAPTER 11 Involve the Audience 157

Task Individuals • Write it Down • Games, Puzzles, and Competitions • Demonstrations • Skits and Role-Plays

CHAPTER 12 Dyads, Triads, Quads, and More 171

Step 1. Set up the Activity • Step 2. Reflect • Step 3. Separate into Smaller Groups • Step 4. Give Instructions • Step 5. Engage • Step 6. Debrief • Adapting to Large Audiences

CHAPTER 13   When Presenting Becomes Facilitating 185

The Facilitator • Develop a Process Agenda • GODA Process Flow

CHAPTER 14   Make Your Message Stick 203

Review and Revisit • Create a Strong, Compelling Call to Action •
Create Accountability • End with the Audience in Mind • Extend the
Conversation

CHAPTER 15   Infuse Your Presentation 213

How to Infuse Your Presentations • Step 1. Do your Homework About
the Audience • Step 2. Lay Out Your Presentation in Bits • Step 3.
Identify Your Objective(s) for Each Bit • Step 4. Note the Current
Techniques • Step 5. Lay Out the Energy Curves • Step 6. Brainstorm
Different Techniques • Step 7. Select the Most Appropriate Technique
• Step 8. Do a Dry Run

CHAPTER 16   Improve Your Presentation Skills 227

Critique Yourself • Self-Assesment Form • Collect Audience Feedback
• Audio/Video Critique • Keep Learning

Conclusion 239

Glossary and Index of Terms 241

Recommended Resources 253

Acknowledgments 257

About the Author 259

FOREWORD

The book you are about to read can have an enormous positive impact on your speaking and presentations in the months and years ahead.

Over the last thirty years, I have delivered more than five thousand presentations, ranging from twenty minutes to five days, to more than five million people from fifty-five countries. In addition, I have read dozens of books on speaking and seminars, and for more than fifteen years I've received high-level professional coaching from people who are considered to be the best in the business.

Then along comes a book like *Boring to Bravo*. As I read through it—page by page and technique by technique—I was once more overwhelmed by how little I know, and how much is still left to learn about this wonderful business of professional speaking and teaching.

Kristin Arnold has written one of the most important books for twenty-first-century speakers, preachers, teachers, trainers, facilitators, and anyone else who has to give a presentation. The methods, techniques, and strategies you will learn in this book are the same ones practiced by those master speakers who bring about powerful and permanent transformations in their audiences.

These methods allow you to connect both emotionally and intellectually with your audiences, affecting them at a deep level and bringing about profound differences in their thoughts, feelings, and subsequent behaviors. As you put these techniques into practice, you will find yourself becoming more positive and persuasive.

Kristin Arnold has a wonderful ability to connect with any audience. Her presentations are inspiring, motivational, and educational—all at once. As a true master of the craft, she is one of the most accomplished and respected speakers, trainers, and facilitators in the world today.

Put up your tray table and fasten your seat belt. Get ready for the next quantum leap in your personal and professional development. What you are about to learn will change your life and the lives of all those people you come in contact with.

—Brian Tracy, CPAE Speaker Hall of Fame
Solana Beach, California

PREFACE

Like you, I have been watching presentations my entire life. Starting with the sermons I heard at the church my family attended and lessons from my schoolteachers, listening to debates while in college and then presentations in the workplace, I have either been thoroughly involved or lulled to sleep. Even many years later, I can still remember the presentations that connected with me, engaged me, and inspired me to action.

After fifteen years in the active duty U.S. Coast Guard, I chose to be a professional facilitator—that is, someone who guides a meeting process and helps a group achieve its desired results in a collaborative fashion. My whole philosophy centers on collaboration, engagement, and participation.

When I entered the world of professional speaking in 1997, I was flabbergasted at the didactic, one-way presentations that seemed to dominate keynote presentations given by professionals and industry experts alike. I just didn't get it. I decided to figure out what makes a presentation go from being ho-hum to awe inspiring. I did an enormous amount of research—reading, watching, and distilling best practices of great, engaging speakers—to create a compendium of techniques I referred to as "Interaction Insights." That collection served as the precursor to this book. My colleagues at the U.S. National Speakers Association (NSA-US) encouraged me to broaden my scope and make it available to the corporate marketplace, which still desperately needs such advice. After another year of diligent research, here is *Boring to Bravo*.

Although my inspiration comes from my NSA-US friends and colleagues, this book would never have made it to print if it wasn't for the cheerleaders in my life: Meg LaBorde Kuehn, who emphatically told me to write this book; Ian Percy, who gave me an Infinite Possibilities pendant that seems to make writing easier; Chris Clarke-Epstein, who always inspires me to write better; my Amazon sister Sarah Michel and all the contributors who graciously shared their perspectives and techniques. By far, my biggest cheerleaders and ultimate fans are my family: the love of my life, Joseph; my son, Travis, who inspires me every day; and my daughter, Marina, who is the coolest person I know.

My hope is that you are able to use this book as a resource to punch up your presentations, taking them from boring monologues to more engaging and interactive dialogues with your audiences.

INTRODUCTION

Bill, the curmudgeonly vice president of manufacturing, had just finished a speech to culminate a three-day facilitation skills workshop. Looking around me at the participants' faces, I could see that they were not impressed. Their course evaluations lambasted his presentation.

It was my duty as the instructor to tell Bill the bad news, especially since he was scheduled to deliver the same presentation the following month. As I showed him the evaluations, Bill looked shocked. "I told them what they needed to know and what I expected them to do with this investment we made in their professional development. What more do you want?"

"The content of your presentation was first-rate, Bill," I agreed. "But the evaluations clearly state that you didn't engage them. Your presentation was a one-way data dump of all the stuff *you* wanted to tell *them*. They didn't want a monologue. They wanted a dialogue with you. They wanted you to talk about what *they* care about."

Bill stammered, "I can see your point, but you gave me only thirty minutes, and I had to cover more information than I had time for. I don't have time to do those stupid, turn-to-your-neighbor kind of activities." Then he crossed his arms in defiance.

Unfortunately, Bill's technique is not atypical of many executives, managers, and salespeople in the workplace. They stand and deliver content to an audience that is vastly different from a few years ago. Today's audiences want more than a talking head. They want to be engaged and involved as you share the content of your presentation.

You, the presenter, may ignore this shift, but it will be at your own peril. Or, you may read on to learn precisely *how* audiences are different and *what is getting in your way* to keep you from being more engaging and interactive.

TODAY'S AUDIENCES ARE DIFFERENT

When I began my professional speaking career more than fifteen years ago, more than 90 percent of the people in the audience were Baby Boomers (those born between 1945 and 1960). The rest were the Silent Traditionalists (born between 1922 and 1944). As a whole, that group was attentive, polite, and respectful. Even if people didn't agree with me, they would passively listen and ask a question or two at the end.

Boomers are now giving way to the younger generations: Generation X (those born between 1961 and 1980) has ascended to midmanagement and fills half of the seats in the audience; Generation Y (born between 1981 and 2001) is coming into the workforce; the Millennials (born after 2002) are sneaking into the back row.

For the first time in history, four generations are working together in one of the most dynamic of times. Conditioned by their experiences at home, in school, and watching cable television, and with their comfort level with ever-changing technology, Gen X and Gen Y members *expect* to be involved, and they are dragging Baby Boomers and Traditionalists along with them.

SCHOOL. Younger generations have grown up with a wider variety of opportunities to engage in their learning. They use computers and access the Internet in their classrooms, they work on team-based projects, they rotate classes and have different teachers, and they have lots of hands-on experiences.

TELEVISION. The media's impact has created generations that struggle to focus for long periods. Starting with *Sesame Street*, the younger generations are used to a variety of vignettes to stimulate their interest. Commercials break up the show every six to eight minutes. Add the multitude of media options at their fingertips, and they are less tolerant of limited programming options. If they don't like what they see, they flip to another channel. So, it should be no surprise that if you don't grab their attention in the first minutes, they will tune you out as well.

GOOGLE. Once upon a time, knowledge was power, to be conveyed in the spoken or written word. Since the 1990s, knowledge is a keystroke away on Google or Wikipedia. Your audience's lives are full of instant updates and news on their cell phones. These younger generations expect speakers to bring specific knowledge about who they are as a group and to be able to convey their expertise in an engaging way—far beyond what they can download off the Internet. Because the world is changing so dramatically, Gen Xers and Yers want to know that you have kept up with your content and with the way they want to take in information. If you stand in front of a lectern and read your notes (even if they are brilliant), you are dead on arrival.

WE'RE ALL SPECIAL. As children, Boomers were raised to be seen and not heard. The younger generations, on the other hand, have been raised in Mr. Rogers's neighborhood, where everyone is seen as *special.* Every kid on the soccer team got a trophy—even if they didn't play! As a result, each and every person in your audience wants to feel special and connected to you.

COMPETITION. You are competing not only with movies whose producers spent $100 million on special effects but also a plethora of presentations accessible on YouTube.com. Why should a younger audience listen to you? It is certainly not because of the artistic quality of your PowerPoint slides or handouts (otherwise, you would be a graphic artist). Your differentiator will be in how you engage and involve them in the presentation.

Soon, these younger generations will be the largest part of your audience, and they don't want to be lectured to. Out of respect, they will pretend to listen quietly, zone out, and surreptitiously pull out their BlackBerries or iPhones to check e-mail or tweet others to comment on how boring you are.

Interestingly enough, this behavior isn't isolated to just Gens X and Y. Baby Boomers are just as willing to pull out their BlackBerries if you don't engage them in a meaningful way. Rather than remind them to put their cell phones away or on vibrate, why not embrace the cell phone as a way to engage the audience? It's much easier to join 'em than to fight 'em! (See more in chapter 6.)

DIVERSITY. Audiences today represent a more diverse cultural workforce than ever before. This presents speakers with more of a challenge to communicate effectively across all kinds of borders, including cultural, ethnic, sexual, religious, and gender differences. Regardless of their packaging, your audiences are expecting you to recognize, understand, and respect their unique perspectives and contributions.

ADULT LEARNING STYLES. We know that adults learn better when exposed to visual, aural, and kinesthetic experiences. They learn, retain, and embrace new information more willingly when they participate in the learning. People learn best when their fingerprints are all over it. Your challenge is to help them imprint their learning so they can apply it to their lives.

TECHNOLOGY. Your audiences are expecting up-to-date, cutting-edge information they can't get elsewhere. They are expecting more than a regurgitated book report; they can get that on the Internet. Your presentation must also capture the human dimension of caring, connecting, and having a conversation—even if you are using the latest and greatest meeting technologies.

Keep in mind, these new technologies are evolving as fast as I type this sentence! Because these technologies simply enable a presenter to reach out to others—especially those not physically present in the room—I opted *not* to put specific online resources in this book. When you see this icon $\mathcal{O}$, you can go to my website, www.BoringToBravo.com, to find links to the most up-to-date resources on the Internet. In the meantime, it is your responsibility to stay current on what is available and look for ways to ultimately engage and involve your audiences, either face-to-face (F2F) or remotely. And, as much as we like our new toys, the simple fact is, if you can't engage F2F, you will definitely have an even harder time connecting with remote locations using technology.

Throw all these factors together and you have a stark reality: In the world of F2F presentations, you don't have a choice. You *must* reach out, connect with the participants, and have meaningful conversations with them in order to be heard, to be remembered, and to inspire them to action.

UNDERSTANDING THE UNDER-30 CROWD

Eric Chester, CSP, CPAE Speaker Hall of Fame

Younger people think in DVD mode, not VCR mode. So they don't read the paper from front to back, and they don't take notes from top to bottom. They've been exposed to unlimited choices, they know they can do things in a way that best suits them and get good results, and they expect that the speakers who address them are aware of that. The most recent generation has educated and influenced the older generations like never before. Having been exposed to technology through their kids, and thus conditioned to absorb information in new ways, a greater number of older people now think in a nonlinear fashion.

WHY WE DON'T ENGAGE

If audiences are demanding more engagement, why aren't more presenters more engaging and interactive? Over the years, I have heard several excuses as to why speakers neither engage nor involve their audiences:

- I don't have time.
- It's too hard.
- I'll lose control.
- No one will participate.
- Not everyone is physically in the same room.
- I can't interact in a keynote.
- I could look really stupid up there.
- I already interact!

How many of these excuses have you used? I have heard them all from managers, salespeople, and even professional speakers I have worked with. You have a choice; you can let one or more of these excuses get in the way *or* you can move beyond these objections. This book will give you lots of creative and energizing ways to overcome your fears, engage and involve the audience, and go from boring to bravo!

TOO MUCH TIME. I need more time than I have been allotted, and my outline is already crammed with information. Besides, audience activities will take precious time away from my actual delivery time.

Yes, full-blown "turn to your partner" activities take more time, but you have a wide range of *other* techniques to choose from that can also engage your audience. Depending on which ones you select, you may actually save time and cover similar material while accomplishing a better result because the participants have connected with you on a deeper level. Remember Bill? This was his main issue, but he did get over it once he learned how.

NO TIME TO PLAN. In the hectic corporate workplace, I don't have extra time to think about how to add more engaging activities to my presentation.

Yes, you do. To pepper your presentation with interaction techniques takes just as much time to plan as it does to prepare any well-prepared speech.

If it is a really important speech, you *must* invest the time to infuse your presentation with a variety of engaging and interactive techniques. Chapter 15 is completely devoted to a simple process to make your presentation more engaging and interactive.

IT'S TOO HARD. Can't I just tell people what to do? That seems a lot easier.

Yes, it is easier because you don't know any better. Despite the generation of the presenter, we continue to stand and deliver our presentations simply because it is easier to do. Although they intuitively know better, even Gen X and Gen Y speakers will occasionally fall back to a lecture style or use one or two traditional techniques—especially when the pressure is on. It will always be easier to recite information (one way) than it is to make an engaging speech (two way) that connects with your audience—unless you have the skills to engage and interact with the audience. This book will give you options to choose from so that involving the audience becomes easier for you.

LOSING CONTROL. Audience involvement is risky. I just don't know what the participants will do. How can I keep it focused? And, if some oddball objects, how do I recover?

Those presenters who are solidly grounded in their content will have an easier time letting go. They have confidence in their material, knowing that no matter what comes their way, they will be able to react and respond gracefully and appropriately. If you tend to be inflexible, you probably won't be able to let go completely, but there are still some low-risk techniques you can use without losing control.

PARTICIPANT RELUCTANCE. What if I ask for participation, but no one wants to participate?

Audiences will not respond well if your attempts to involve them are lame. You can't just indiscriminately ask for a show of hands or ask the audience to turn to the person next to them to achieve interactivity. You also can't do something that has no connection to the larger message. To do so is contrived and gimmicky. That is why you need to carefully select the techniques you are going to use. The audience will respond well to you when you show how much you care about them. When you make an effort to connect with them, there will *always* be someone in the crowd who wants to participate with you.

NOT F2F. I can't arrange for participation because everyone isn't physically in the room. The presentation is broadcast to one or more different sites.

This is a great excuse that holds zero water. You absolutely *can* engage and involve smaller audiences in geographically dispersed locations—as long as you *plan* for it. But it won't work if you don't even think about the remote locations or if you try to do it off the cuff. There are simple things you can do to include these remote locations and participants. It is not about the technology; it is all about the planning. Remember that other people are present with you, and you can use the technology to support their involvement.

NOT FOR KEYNOTES. I'm giving a keynote, and you just don't do interaction in a keynote.

Says who? True, the traditional keynote is more didactic, and it is typically given within sixty minutes at either the beginning or the end of a conference about a single, key theme. Who says you can't be engaging and participative, though? Today's audiences are changing. They want to be connected and involved in the program. The least you can do is incorporate a few of these techniques. Mind you, not all of them may work for you or for your audience, but many of them will. The techniques I describe in chapters 12 and 13 might be too risky for you, but I have also seen large group activities and facilitation done with aplomb. Last time I checked, there weren't any keynote police standing at the door, so give it a try.

EMBARRASSED. Since I don't know what they will do (or not do), I could be really humiliated if the activity blows up in my face.

You're right. During a high-risk activity, you could be embarrassed if you haven't thought it through or practiced it once or twice with your friends or colleagues. Keep in mind, however, that most audiences *want you to succeed.* They don't want you to be embarrassed because then they get embarrassed for you! So, if something misfires, look at it as part of the process. You shift to plan B and keep moving on.

STUCK IN A RUT. What are you talking about? I engage the audience all of the time!

Some presenters see no need to change because their traditional approach to speaking has brought them success for years. Even if you think you are already engaging your audiences enough, you may be relying on just a few tried-and-true techniques that work for you. This book will provide a veritable cornucopia of techniques to add variety to your presentations.

Regardless of the excuse, your ability to involve the audience in a more active way requires a different skill set that many presenters have not yet mastered. They may want to, but they don't know how. Although learning how will be challenging, overcoming the obstacles to incorporating interactive techniques in your presentations is well worth the effort.

BORING TO BRAVO

No one wants to be boring. But a stand-and-deliver style of presenting just doesn't work well with today's audiences. This book will give you options. Rather than relying on the one or two techniques you seem to always use, you have in your hands a wide-ranging smorgasbord of techniques you can use *today* to make your current presentations more engaging and interactive. I warn you, though. This is *not* a basic presentation skills book. I have made two assumptions about readers of this book: one, that you have given a speech before, and two, that you have read one or two basic presentation skills books before. If not, check out the recommended resources section at the back of this book. 🔎

Unlike a basic presentation skills book, *Boring to Bravo* will give you practical tools and techniques to engage the audience as well as interact with them.

What is the difference? When you *engage* an audience member, you attract his interest and attention. He shifts from being an attendee to being a listener. When you *interact* with an audience member, you have an effect on her. There is reciprocity between the speaker and the audience. She shifts from being a listener to being a co-participant *with* you.

Where does the engagement leave off and the interaction begin? Seems like a fine point, doesn't it? You can be entertaining and full of life and energy; we would call that being "engaging." Yes, you, the presenter are engaging *to* the audience. An interaction occurs when there is an exchange *between* the presenter and the audience. It can be something as innocuous as an acknowledgment that a person in your audience is smiling at you in knowing appreciation. Or a simple answer to a question. You, the presenter, are involving and interacting *with* the audience.

What makes an engaging speaker more interactive? You *care* about what the audience is thinking and feeling. You make small choices throughout the presentation to continue as planned or to adapt to meet their needs. If you didn't care, you wouldn't be canvassing the room to see if they are with you or not.

Engagement and interaction, then, go hand in hand—and it all depends on your mind-set. To be an interactive presenter, you have to genuinely understand the *audience's* world and *their* needs. You must

- Care about the audience;
- Connect with each member of the audience as an individual participant;
- Converse with your audience; and
- Collaborate with the participants.

In chapter 1, I discuss in greater detail the importance of having this mind-set.

Chapters 2–14 describe the smorgasbord of techniques you can use to engage and involve the audience, not only during your presentation but also before and after. The techniques listed are not the *definitive* list, but they are, nevertheless, a treasure trove of possibilities to use during any kind of presentation, no matter how formal or informal, and no matter how long—whether just a few minutes, or an hour, or an entire day. Will you use them all in the same presentation? No, I hope not!

As you read through this book the first time, you will identify a few techniques you rely on all of the time. Good for you! There's nothing like a little reinforcement that you are on the right path.

Whether you are a new presenter or a seasoned professional, everyone needs to add a little variety to the mix. Depending on your personality, you can try out a new and unfamiliar technique in a low-risk presentation, or even among some friends. See what works and what doesn't. Then, as you practice, you will adapt the technique to suit your own style and your audience's style. Your success in using these techniques is limited only by your forethought and creativity.

Chapter 15 describes a process by which you can quickly sprinkle these new techniques into your presentation or deliberately insert them at critical moments in your speech. You will want to keep this book handy as a reference tool to inspire new techniques of your own and to help you create engaging and interactive presentations.

I have assigned a "risk rating" to each technique, which gauges how risky the technique is, from low risk (⚠) to highly risky (⚠ ⚠ ⚠ ⚠ ⚠). Depending on your risk tolerance, or if you don't know the audience very well, start out with a low-risk technique; as participants begin to trust you, you can select other techniques with a higher risk rating.

Chapter 16 focuses on improving your presentation skills. I assure you, fewer than 20 percent of presenters actually go through the rigor of continuously improving their platform skills. Look at the table of contents in most books on presentation skills and you'll see they barely mention how to increase your expertise and eloquence on the platform. This final chapter lets you bring all of your insights together to create a plan to improve your presentations.

This book is structured to give you a little help in that regard. At the end of each chapter you'll find a recap that uses a different technique to highlight the main points in that chapter. Additionally, there is space for you to write your own reflections: What should you continue doing? Start doing? Stop doing? Since you have made the investment of money and time in purchasing and reading this book, I encourage you to continue the learning journey and fill out the chapter recaps as you read.

So, are you ready to start your journey from boring to bravo? I am delighted that you have joined me. Read chapter 1 and then feel free to skip around within chapters 2 through 14. When you feel that you have a good command of the techniques, read chapters 15 and 16.

From this point forward, I promise that you will never watch TV, listen to the radio, or read a magazine article without jotting down a technique or commenting on how the presenter is engaging or interacting with his or her audiences. It's habit forming! And when you see something of note, make a comment on my blog at www.BoringToBravo.com or drop me an e-mail at Kristin@BoringToBravo.com. Let me know how your next presentation goes as you make it more engaging and interactive!

HAVE AN ENGAGING MIND-SET

JANE, A NEWLY PROMOTED VP in a Fortune 500 company, was the one who kicked off the annual departmental goal-setting session. For fifteen minutes, she stood at the front of the room and pontificated her perspective on the team's purpose and her expectations. That quarter hour was an eternity to the rest of us in the room. By the end of her rambling presentation, she had subconsciously dragged an empty chair from the side of the room and blockaded herself from the rest of us. There were no questions, and we dutifully thanked her for "setting the tone." Unfortunately, she set the tone for numbness, not collaboration on the department's goals. As the group's professional facilitator, I was hoping Jane's opening comments would inspire her folks rather than put a damper on their enthusiasm.

When I chatted with Jane just a few days before the session, she was visibly excited about the upcoming meeting. If only she had been able to share the same engaging "presentation" she gave me then with her employees! What happened between our informal conversation and her actual presentation? In talking with Jane later, she agreed that she hadn't come into her speech with a focused, engaging mind-set. Something urgent had cropped up and she got distracted. Jane just wanted to get through the departmental meeting and back to putting out the fire.

Your attitude is intuitively felt by your audience, and they mirror whatever you bring into the presentation right back to you. If you are engaged, they will be too. If you are having fun, they will have fun as well. If you are distracted and preoccupied with something else, they will turn their attention elsewhere.

Audience engagement starts with you. You have the ability to *create* an engaging audience, and it starts with the mind-set you have about this activity we call a "presentation."

IT'S ABOUT THEM, NOT ABOUT YOU

Giving a speech is one of the most stressful responsibilities you have in the workplace, especially if you do not give presentations routinely. It is easy to get caught up in the moment, thinking, "Will I make sense? Do I look all right? Am I going to embarrass myself?"

To be an effective, engaging presenter, you have to let go of your own internal conversations and focus on your audience. This means you have to *care* sincerely about and want to *connect* with each person in the audience. They need to know that you are putting their needs *first*. That means you need to know enough about them so they feel they can trust you and will want to listen to you.

RESEARCH. We all despise the speaker who delivers his presentation on autopilot, never changing a word. It is the same presentation for one audience as it is for a completely different audience. To engage an audience, a presenter needs to find out their hopes, fears, and interests. Take the time to understand the people, their backgrounds, and the collective culture—often called the "personality" of the group—so you can connect your comments with what they care about.

CONTENT. The actual message you share should address the issues that your audience cares about, not the ones you *think* they should care about. This is a subtle distinction with dramatic implications. If you do not address something that helps them make their lives better or improves the life of someone they care about, you are dead on arrival.

MAKE IT PERSONAL. Few things can help you bond and establish a connection with a group better than knowing and using people's names.

- Obtain a participant list ahead of time and read through the list out loud several times. If possible, learn the correct pronunciation of the difficult names.

- As you meet a new participant, say her name quietly to yourself a few times and make any associations that will help you recall the name later.

- With a small audience (and only if time permits), have each person share their name at the beginning of your program. As you listen to the introductions, silently recall their names.

- Make a small seating chart that you can refer to.

- Arrange for nametags or table tents with first names in large type.

- As quickly as possible in your presentation, begin using first names when addressing individuals in the audience.

MORE "WE" THAN "ME." If you are truly focused on the audience, you will use more inclusive language. Rather than saying "I did this" and "Look at me," you will inherently talk more about them, using either the words "you" or "we." Which would you rather hear: "My client is . . ." or "You might have a client like this . . ."? It's a subtle difference, yet it invites participation rather than making it all about you, the presenter.

LISTEN. As you are speaking, shift your focus from how *you* are doing to how the *audience* is doing. When you "listen" to the audience, you are much more aware of their verbal and nonverbal reactions during your speech. Are they smiling and nodding their heads? Yes; you are in the zone. Puzzled looks? Hmm; you may want to share an example or an illustration. Are they paying attention to you or looking at their BlackBerries? Are they leaning forward in their chairs or sitting back defensively? Do they respond to your witticisms, your questions, and your stories, or are their eyes glazed over?

ADJUST. As you listen to your audience, you can either continue as planned or adapt your speech. Because you aren't going to hit the mark all the time, always prepare a plan B to pull out of your back pocket. Audiences are quite forgiving as long as they know you care about them. They want you to succeed. So if one technique doesn't work, try another until you do connect.

EXPERIMENT:
USING INCLUSIVE LANGUAGE

During one of your presentations, have someone tally the number of times you use a personal pronoun and some form of the words "you" and "we." The ratio of the number of times you use inclusive language versus the times you use the imperial "me" and "I" should, at a minimum, be 2:1. Ideally, you should aim for 4:1. Remember, it's all about them, not you!

Please count the number of times I use these words during my presentation from the moment I start my program to the point where I begin speaking about "using inclusive language."

		Total
Personalize using a person's name		
You, yours		
We, ours, us		
I, mine, me, my		
Total		

BE PASSIONATE

It is hard *not* to like a person who is passionate about her topic and focuses her comments on what the participants need to know. If you are passionate about a topic, your interest in the topic will come through loud and clear and engage all the folks in the audience.

BE INTERESTED. If you want others to be interested in what you say, you should be excited about it too. Even if it is the most boring topic on the planet, figure out what makes it interesting and how the participants may be affected by this topic. There is always something you can dig up that will pique your interest as well as your audience's.

BELIEVE. You must believe in what you are saying, without any reservation. If you don't believe it, don't present it. Your audiences can detect a poser in a heartbeat.

KNOW YOUR STUFF. Be a master of your topic with a depth of knowledge that clearly exceeds your audience's knowledge about the subject. Especially when you are involving the audience in higher-risk techniques, you must be so well-grounded that you can bounce back from any situation.

MAKE IT YOURS. Even if you are handed a slide show to present, make it yours. Do something that can improve, enlarge, or enlighten the core idea. Insert a few techniques from this book so you can feel your imprint on the presentation.

LET IT SHOW. Don't be afraid to show your passion. Many speakers try to look ultra professional and keep a little distance between themselves and their audience. We tend to restrict our gestures, our voice, as well as our enthusiasm when we should be doing the exact opposite! Unless you are already a bouncing bundle of energy, give yourself permission to let your natural enthusiasm shine through.

BE YOURSELF

Everything that makes you unique—your quirky sense of humor, your stylish appearance, and your unusual stories—makes you an engaging speaker. Never doubt that you have what it takes to engage an audience. People gravitate toward a real, genuine, and authentic speaker, not someone who is emulating some other great orator or adopting another person's material. Authentic presenters speak about real-world experiences they are passionate about. When you are authentic, the audience knows it; they respond better and open up to you.

HAVE CONFIDENCE. You have mastered the content and you have a solid process to engage and involve the audience. Don't get too cocky, but be confident in who you are and what you are doing. People want to know that they are in good hands.

CARE. Demonstrate or articulate how you genuinely care about the people in the room. In many small and meaningful ways, let them know how much you care, and they will care about what you say.

BE HONEST. There are times when you get asked the tough question or you find yourself on the spot. If you can, answer the question honestly and gracefully, without excuses or defenses. If you are unable to answer the question, be honest about that too. Your audience will respect you for your honesty more than for your attempts to fake an answer or an attitude.

BE HUMBLE. No one cares for a guru who pontificates from on high. Let your audience know that you are a mere mortal and have struggled with the same issues they have. A little self-disclosure goes a long way.

BE PRESENT. Unlike Jane, whom you met at the beginning of this chapter, you must be firmly rooted in the moment, participating with the audience, attentive to their needs, wants, and moods. You are not thinking about what might happen five minutes after the meeting ends. You are completely attuned to the here and now. When you give your audience your undivided attention, they give it back to you!

BE SPONTANEOUS. When you are in the moment, you can adapt your presentation easily, building on what was said earlier, reacting to real-time situations, and interacting with the participants.

BE TRANSPARENT. When something goes wrong—which, at some point, it will—acknowledge it and ask the audience what to do about it. If you lose your train of thought, which we all do at some time or another, tell the group and self-correct, either by taking a deep breath and focusing or asking the audience to remind you where you left off. Whatever happens, do not try to cover it up, gloss it over, or pretend it never happened. It did, the audience knows it, and they might even be able to help you solve it. It is no longer embarrassing once everyone knows.

HAVE FUN. Although giving a presentation is inherently stressful, try to enjoy yourself. If you have fun, then the people in the room will too. If you aren't having fun, it's a sure bet they aren't either.

EXPERIMENT: WHAT MAKES YOU UNIQUE?

Ask your friends and coworkers this simple question: "As a presenter, what makes me unique?" Then, just be quiet and let them respond. Take notes. Ask questions for clarification but *do not* answer them. Just take in the data. After you do this a few times, you will see some themes recur. Is this description the real you? Or is there some other facet of your personality you want to show more?

HAVE A CONVERSATION

Whether you are speaking to a few people or to a packed auditorium, present your information in a conversational style rather than a stilted "this is how presenters present" style. Most of us are pretty engaging when we speak one-on-one or to a small group of close friends. So why not take that comfortable, casual style with you onto the stage or to the front of the room? Your local television news anchors and reporters have a more conversational tone, and so can you.

CONNECT. Strive to make your speech a personal conversation with everyone in the room by connecting with audience members individually. When you start your presentation, find a friendly face. If you know the person (or you can see the person's nametag), you can address that individual by name as you would in an informal conversation. When you finish one train of thought, find another friendly face. Then have a chat with that new person.

CHAT. Think of your conversation as a series of small chats with different members of the audience. When you chat *with* someone, you simply can't have a one-way transmission of data. Instead, there is a verbal and nonverbal exchange between you and the person you are chatting with, plus each and every member of your audience.

CLEAN IT UP. Be careful about being too chatty, however. Our informal conversations can sometimes sputter, ramble, and lead us down a rabbit trail. They are full of wild gestures, meaningless words, and vocalized hiccups like "um," "er," "ah," and "you know." Audiences will expect you to be as chatty and as eloquent as the personalities they see on television. Speak the way you normally do, but with a tad more intentionality about what you say and how you say it.

COLLABORATE WITH THEM

If you want to involve the audience at a deeper level, you can move beyond just a conversation to collaborate with the participants. Because you care and have connected, a collaborative mind-set is established, and the audience will do what you ask them to do. Once you set the process in motion, the wisdom within the crowd will create something better than anything you could—in large part because they created it. Their fingerprints will be all over it. When the audience creates the outcome, they have more ownership in actually carrying it to completion.

Collaboration gets dicey for some people, and frankly, some people just cannot let go of being the sage on the stage. When you collaborate with the audience, it only *feels* like you lose a bit of control—not knowing where the audience is going to go, how they will respond, or how you can get them back on track. If you have a firm grasp of the *process*, it becomes much easier to let go of the content.

It starts with an outcome, that is, the reason you are giving the presentation. You design a process that takes them on a journey where they discover their own "aha!" You are not really the presenter sharing your insights; you are more of a facilitator who guides the process (see chapter 13).

LET THEM CHOOSE. Allow the participants to set the agenda, select the best choice, determine the path forward, discern the next steps, assess the situation, and so forth. As much as you can, give them options where they can choose where they want to go.

ASK FOR INVOLVEMENT. Bob Pike, a renowned champion of participant-centered training, says, "Never do for your audience what they can do for themselves." Unless you ask the audience to do something, they will be passive, compliant listeners. Turn them into active, engaged participants by asking them to do something. The more collaborative speakers reach deep into their repertoire to involve the participants as much as they can in unusual and surprising ways.

BE SPONTANEOUS. When you collaborate, you must be quick on your feet, able to go with the flow, and be spontaneous with the audience. When you know your content thoroughly and you have thought through the process (along with a plan B for when things go wrong), you can deal with anything that comes your way.

TRUST. Once you put the process in motion, get out of the way. Let the participants follow the process so they can bump into their own magical moments of discovery and enlightenment. Their moments may not be the ones you predicted or even your own revelations, but be assured, they will be meaningful to the audience, and that's what counts in the end.

THE GLOBAL TRENDS TOWARD CONNECTION AND INVOLVEMENT

Brad MacMillan, C.A., president, and CEO of Meeting Professionals International (MPI)

Two of the biggest trends happening in businesses all over the world are collaboration and personalization. These two trends are having profound effects on the meeting experience in particular, because it's not good enough now just to have a topic and say, "Here's what I know, and here's what I have been working with for years, and here is what you need to know." It doesn't work like that anymore. Audiences' expectations have evolved so much past that mind-set; if we are not considering how to personalize the experience and actually collaborate with our constituencies we will not be successful.

The number one thing that an audience wants is to feel involved in the actual creation and development of the session. When they are involved, they are much more connected, they feel it is more personal to them, and they get more out of it.

Now let me give you an example. When Don Tapscott, author of the best seller *Wikinomics*, was our keynote speaker at MPI, he did a great job in advance of reaching out to all of our attendees. He blogged with them, invited questions before the event, and considered them; he built them right into his presentation. So, in essence, he built his presentation around the interests of his audience even before they got there. The audience felt like they were personally involved. They felt like they could see their fingerprints all over the content he delivered. And so they got more out of it. And Don went the extra step and engaged with people after the fact, too. It really was an end-to-end experience. It was personal, and the people who were in the audience felt that they had collaborated and created something remarkable.

PREPARE FOR INEVITABLE RESISTANCE

I was sitting in the back of the training room watching a fellow professional speaker give a presentation on retention strategies. After her opening remarks, she asked us to break into small groups to discuss the biggest challenge we were having retaining people. A big, burly man looked at me and growled: "I don't do small groups. I came to hear what *she* has to say, not what *you* have to say about it."

He had a point. Even though adult learning theory tells us that men and women will retain more information if they are involved in their own learning, many seated in the audience—especially the Baby Boomers—are more comfortable with the old presentation paradigm, which merely requires them to sit back and listen.

You can count on it; some people are just going to resist getting involved. Don't take it personally; it is a normal, natural part of the process. You can increase their participation, however, with these five distinct strategies.

CHANGE EXPECTATIONS. There are a slew of techniques you can use to set the tone for interaction even before your audience walks into the room (see chapter 2). Those who still don't want to participate will either opt out or sit in the back of the room.

THERE'S ALWAYS SOMEONE WHO WON'T BE HAPPY!

Kit Grant, CSP, HoF Speaker Hall of Fame

As a keynote presenter, I discovered the best way to fend off these unwanted and potentially damaging audience reactions is to "pre-call" as many of the customary objections as possible, preferably in the opening remarks when I set the stage for what's to come.

Here are a few I've found to be effective, based on my style (which is not particularly touchy-feely):

1. I explain very early in the presentation I am not there to be liked—I am there to make them think about the message. I warn them that in doing so, some people may be offended, so everyone should be prepared. For the few who really enjoy being offended, this presentation could be the highlight of the entire event.

2. I tell them what I will and will not do. I expect their involvement, but I won't bring people up on stage or make them do some uncomfortable interactive exercise with people they don't know. This usually puts them at ease.

3. I suggest they may have some fun and jokingly warn them that if I see they are not having any I may come out in the audience and confront them on the spot. I wouldn't do that, of course, but it keeps them on their toes!

PREEMPT OBJECTIONS. You know what the objections will be, so address them up front. For example, if you want audience members to share ideas with their neighbors, you can say, "I know you are thinking, 'I don't know that person.' Well, now is a good time to meet a new face, so say hello and share your idea!" By voicing their objections, it gives them permission to act.

MAKE IT OKAY. Even if you have set the tone and preempted their objections, a few may still not want to play. That's okay; that is their *choice*. You don't need 100 percent participation. In fact, the best participation is voluntary rather than gained through pressure or intimidation. Even though some may not play by your rules, they are still participating in their own way.

RECOGNIZE PHYSICAL LIMITATIONS. Be aware of anything that might limit someone's ability to participate, and adjust appropriately. The most common obstacle you will face is the room configuration, which we will discuss in chapter 2. Keep in mind that you can also have participant limitations. For example, don't take a straw poll by asking people to raise their hands if there is a participant with no arms. No kidding, I have actually seen this happen! Ask for a verbal response instead.

BE TRANSPARENT. If there is something going on in the crowd but it's obvious only to you, you may not need to say anything. If it is obvious to everyone in the room, and is therefore a distraction, you cannot ignore it. You need to acknowledge what is happening. Either calmly deal with it or ask the audience for help. A simple example would be a projector malfunction. Don't get flustered. Tell the audience what is going on and ask for help to fix it, or forge ahead without it.

 Don't forget to check out more resources and downloads at www.boringtobravo.com.

CHAPTER ONE RECAP

 You have the ability to create an engaging audience, starting with the mind-set you have about your presentation. To be engaging, sincerely care about the audience, reach out and connect with them, and make what you say a conversation about them, not about you.

- Do your research about your audience.
- Know what the participants care about.
- Make it personal.
- Use inclusive language.
- Be genuinely and uniquely "you."
- Listen to your audience as you are speaking.
- Adjust your behaviors in real time if you are not connecting.

ACTION PLAN

Based on the information in this chapter, I intend to

Continue _____

Start _____

Stop _____

CHAPTER TWO

SET AN INTERACTIVE TONE

YOUR PRESENTATION STARTS the moment you know that you will be giving a speech. And from that moment forward, you can do a number of things to set the tone for engagement and interaction—*before* you stand at the front of the room or on the stage.

Think about the last presentation you attended. When you walked into the room, what did you notice? How did you feel? What were you expecting to happen? Did it happen the way you expected?

When your audience walks into the room, they want to know that they are in good hands. They want to know that they are in the right place and feel connected not only to the topic but also to the presenter and the other people in the room.

At the onset, you can create the expectation that you will do more than just talk *at* them. You are going to *engage* them and *connect with* them in a meaningful way. But it doesn't happen just because you wish it so. You must put a little forethought into how you are going to set the tone for the entire presentation.

REACH OUT AND CONNECT WITH YOUR AUDIENCE ⚠ ⚠

Even before you walk into the meeting room, you can reach out and connect with the people who are planning on attending your presentation. Here are some proven ideas on how to reach out and connect:

INTERVIEW. Pick up the phone or visit a few of your potential participants. Ask the meeting planner for the names and contact information for three "influencers" or "heavy hitters"—that is, those who are very visible, well-known, and respected within the audience. Arrange to meet these leaders and other audience members of the audience prior to your speech. Ask them what they would like to hear about, what challenges they are facing, and who is a "star"—someone in the audience or in the company who performs your topic extremely well. You can also ask them about any specific jargon, acronyms, or terminology peculiar to the group that you should be aware of. You can weave elements of all of this fabulous information *about them* into your presentation.

SURVEY. E-mail the participants a quick, Web-based survey: "In order to make the day most relevant to your needs, you can begin participating with me now. Would you take this Web-based survey or e-mail me one or more questions you would like to have addressed during the presentation? Not to worry, I won't single you out when I address your question."

PREWORK. Is there something the attendees can read or do in preparation for your speech? Ask them to think about the topic or a specific scenario. Give them an interesting article to read. Ask them to do a self-evaluation. One caveat: If you have them do prework, make sure you at least thank them for investing their time in assisting in the preparation of the program.

BLOG. Open up the discussions to all of the participants through a blog wiki or other Internet-based community-building tool. You can post either previews of your discussion or the prework itself and allow the participants to create their own "buzz" before you even walk into the room.

E-MAIL OR VOICE MAIL BLAST. Some organizations have the ability to blast a voice mail or e-mail to all the participants encouraging them to attend the session. You can also record an audio track that starts playing when you open up your e-mail. Now that's a splendid opportunity to send a strong audible signal that your presentation will be energizing and engaging.

TEASER. At the meeting venue, set out a flyer, post a few signs, or use another promotional gimmick to entice participants to check out your session (rather than someone else's). Michael Soon Lee, marketing expert in selling to people from diverse cultures, prints out a bunch of "admission tickets" to his event and places them all over the conference center. "What made it so effective is that I paid the night manager of the convention hotel to slip one under the door of every registered attendee so they were there when people woke up. The next day everyone was abuzz asking how I managed to accomplish this. It's amazing what a $25 tip will do!"

BLACK BELT NEGOTIATING™

ADMIT ONE

FOR SPEAKERS

FEBRUARY 16
4:15 - 5:30 PM
GRAND BALLROOM H - J

You don't want to miss the ending!

PRESENTER: MICHAEL SOON LEE, CSP

IDENTIFY "PARTICIPANTS." If your presentation will include a demonstration, skit, role-play, or other interaction that requires advance planning, get together with the meeting planner to identify specific participants who will be able to interact appropriately.

IDENTIFY THE "EXPERTS." Every once in a while, someone in the audience thinks they know more than you do about the topic and that they should be giving the speech. If you know about these experts in advance, you can talk to them prior to the presentation to prevent any potential sharp-shooting. You may even want to consider referring to their expertise at some point in your presentation.

INVOLVE YOUR AUDIENCE WELL IN ADVANCE

Kim Snider

An easy technique to involve your audience is to ask them, in advance, what their biggest questions or concerns are around the presentation topic. Then build the presentation around their responses. By definition, you will have a highly relevant presentation for your audience. Are they going to attend when they know you are going to address their specific issue? You bet!

This technique is quite simple to implement. Whether you automate the process or do it manually will depend on how often you present and to how many people. It can be as simple as sending participants an e-mail in advance and asking them to e-mail back their response. If you are doing webinars for the public, for example, and have a registration system on your website, you may want to use this as part of your confirmation e-mail. If you do a lot of presentations on the same topic and to different groups, you may want to set up a Web page that uses a survey site to collect the responses. 🔎 You can also create a simple database on your Web server and collect the answers there; however, this solution will likely require some help from your Web developer.

Once you collect the responses, what do you do with them? Here are a few ideas:

♦ Circulate themes in advance to stimulate thought and additional ideas.

♦ Use the common themes in your presentation reminder and follow-up e-mail.

♦ Show the laundry list of questions and concerns early in the presentation.

♦ Quote verbatim from the survey responses during the presentation.

♦ Use the ideas generated from the survey responses as ideas for white papers, articles, or blog posts to mention during and follow up on after the presentation.

Bottom line: Don't wait until the presentation starts to engage your audience. Engage them early, make your presentation all about them, and you are much more likely to hit the mark.

GRAB 'EM WITH A LIVELY TITLE ⚠ ⚠

The title of your presentation is your first chance to capture your audience's attention. An intriguing title signals your intent to be lively and engaging instead of dull and boring. A catchy and effective title should

- Be appropriate to the occasion or tie into the conference theme
- Provide enough information about the subject so that potential attendees can tell whether this is likely to be of interest to them
- Be succinct and to the point
- Pique the interest of the reader or potential listener

Perhaps you are like me: I acknowledge that I need a lively title, but I can't always think of one! My colleague, Sam Horn, is renowned for helping individuals and organizations create intriguing ideas and original approaches that help them break out versus blend in. I asked her to share three techniques you can use to create a catchy title. Here's what she has to say.

CREATE THE PERFECT TITLE

Sam Horn

Identify your P.O.D. (Points of Distinction). What is a common truth about your topic? Don't bore people by featuring that in your title or description. Saying the same thing as everyone else is a prescription for blending in. And blending in is for Cuisinarts, not for presenters. How can you say the opposite instead of the obvious? A presentation entitled "The Customer is NOT Always Right" that delves into how employees can deal with chronic complainers who consistently break the rules is more likely to elicit interest. Many people would welcome what promises to be a "tell-it-like-it-is" presentation that address a real problem without a Pollyanna approach.

NURD a New Word. Use a POP! technique called "Alphabetizing" to coin a NURD (my word for a New Word). Are you going to run right out and sign up for a workshop on economics? Probably not. However, run that word through the alphabet, playing with different pronunciations and spellings; aconomics, beconomics, ceconomics, deconomics, economics, feconomics . . . wait a minute . . . how about Freakonomics? You may be thinking, "Big deal, so it's a clever name." You bet it's a big deal. Levy and Dubner have turned that innovative title into an extremely successful corporate keynote, a best-selling book, and a thriving consulting practice.

How can you do this? Write down twenty words you frequently use when describing your topic. Now take each of those words and run it through the alphabet until you come up with an option that POP!s (that's Purposeful, Original, and Pithy).

Half and Half. On a fresh piece of paper, draw a vertical line down the center. Now start describing your topic, "It's half this and half this," placing some words on the left and some on the right. Now, start mixing and matching the words, blending the first half of a word with the last half of another word until something clicks.

I've used this technique to help many clients create brands that have catapulted their careers. For example, Christine Martinello was one of many speakers addressing the challenge women professionals have juggling work and home life, their duties as a mom and a manager—MOMager, a brand that has helped her be one-of-a-kind.

What's this mean for you? You've probably invested days, weeks, or maybe even months developing and polishing the content in your presentation. Now spend time crafting an intriguing title for that presentation so people are motivated to show up and be prepared to be engaged.

Excerpted from *POP! Create the Perfect Pitch, Title and Tagline for Anything!* [Perigee-Penguin, 2009]. Used with permission.

BUILD ON THE MEETING THEME ⚠ ⚠

"There is something in the air." Steve Jobs opened up Macworld 2008 with those words and set the theme for his presentation to introduce the ultrathin MacBook Air laptop. The "air" theme weaved its way throughout his presentation, culminating in Jobs pulling the Air computer out of a manila envelope.

Think of your theme as the glue that holds your speech together. While it can be the purpose of your talk, it can also be a recurring or pervasive idea that you can get the audience to remember and even to participate in.

If the meeting doesn't have a theme, try creating your own. For example, if you are doing a team-building session, you can choose a sports theme. (Oh, come on, *everybody* does a sports theme for team building. You can be more creative than that.) Or try a Go West! theme for the tough journey the team is going to be making. Or pick a different theme that suits the audience and the objective.

Once you select your theme, brainstorm ways to tangibly infuse the theme into your speech. Here are some ideas to trigger your imagination using both our sports and Western themes:

- Props

  - Use a referee's whistle or a rustler's triangle to bring the group back together at the end of a small group activity.

  - Group people by different sports balls (baseballs, basketballs, footballs, soccer balls) or by different color bandanas.

  - Reward participants with theme-appropriate "prizes" of sports or cowboy paraphernalia.

- Visuals

  - Post pictures/graphics of the different sports balls or colors to indicate the location of each subgroup in the room.

  - Pepper your presentation with theme-inspired graphics.

- Music

  - Play recorded team "fight songs" or popular spaghetti Western soundtracks or country-and-western songs to create the mood as participants enter the room.

- Costumes

  - Encourage the participants to come dressed to match the theme in their favorite sports team's colors/jerseys or cowboy/Western wear.

  - Get into the spirit and come dressed to match the theme (as a referee, a football player, a cheerleader, or cowboy/cowgirl). Just make sure you are still dressed professionally!

INTERACTIVE TONE

MAKE THE ROOM
MORE ENGAGING ⚠

You walk into the meeting room at least a half hour before your presentation, maybe more if you are using technology. You take a good look around the room. Yep. There are tables, chairs, a projector, and a screen. Sigh. Don't all these meeting rooms look just about the same? Boring.

Don't be afraid to change it up to send the signal that this talk is not going to be your typical, ho-hum presentation. Part of caring is paying attention to room conditions. Regardless of who has control over the room temperature, sound quality, or other environmental issues, *you* are ultimately responsible for the audience's experience. No one else. Find out the room logistics prior to your presentation and set the room so the participants will be able to easily connect with you and with each other.

ROOM SIZE. If you have any say in the matter, try to get a room large enough to hold the expected number of attendees—and nothing bigger. When you have 50 people in a room that can seat 150, your participants will spread out, leaving lots of space between tiny clusters of people. It will be much more difficult to create connections with small groups scattered from one end of the room to the other. If you have to choose between a room that is slightly too small and one that is slightly too large, choose the smaller room with standing room only.

SEATING ARRANGEMENTS. To allow participants to comfortably accomplish the activities you have in mind, set the chairs so they can be close to you and to each other.

- Align the front of the room along the longest wall, with the entrance doors to the back, so that participants can be closer to you. A long and narrow room makes everyone feel like they are in a bowling alley.

- Set up the first row of chairs as close as possible. It creates connection for both you and the attendees.

- Face each chair directly toward the spot you will be presenting from, and make sure each person has an unobstructed view. For example, if you are using theater-style seating (rows of chairs), curve the seating at the end of each row so everyone can see you better.

- Create some "access lanes" down the sides so people can easily move around. Try not to put an access lane down the center of the room, as center aisles tend to drain energy from the presentation.

- Have enough seats for all, but not too many. Usher people toward the front, use yellow police tape to block off the back rows until the front fills up, and keep a few chairs stacked in the back for latecomers.

TABLES. The table configuration you use can support interaction as well:

- Eliminate the small water table that separates you from your audience.

- For small audiences (fewer than twenty-five people), try a U-shaped arrangement where the audience fans out around the speaker on three sides. This enables the presenter to walk into the audience easily and encourages participation not only with the speaker but also with each other.

- Have five to seven people sit at round tables, leaving the side of the table closest to the presenter unoccupied. This means the participants are already divided into clusters for small group activities.

- Do you really need a table at all? Go from boring to bravo and take out the tables!

LIGHTING. Since you are the number one visual, you shouldn't be in the dark—ever. The house lights don't need to be turned down in order for your slides to be visible with most multimedia projectors nowadays. It is a hard habit to break, but if you find yourself in the dark, make sure you have a light source that will spotlight you. Then, mark the stage floor with tape to show your lighting boundaries so you know when you are moving over to the dark side. Don't forget to ask someone to turn the lights back up when you are done with your slide show.

PLATFORM. In audiences of more than a hundred people, you should present from a platform that allows everyone to see you. I know; you don't like speaking from a platform. Get over it. Remember, this is not about *what you want*; it is about *what your audience needs*. And they need to see all of you—not just your head.

SCREEN TO THEIR LEFT. Since we read from left to right, make it easier for the audience to "read" what you are saying by placing the screen to the left of the stage (downstage right in theater terms). Place the screen at the same depth as you will be standing and close enough to your center position that the audience's eyes won't have to travel a great distance from you to the screen. Furthermore, should you have to point to something on the screen, you can use your right hand without turning your back to the participants.

LECTERN. For the same reasons as outlined for your screen placement, set the lectern, if you must have one, to their left (downstage right) so that you can have the center stage free to move about.

NAME BADGES. If you don't know the names of the people in the audience, check with the meeting planner to see if the participants will be wearing name badges or have name tents. If so, encourage the planner to print the first name of each person in LARGE capital letters, so you can address people by their first name.

POSTERS. Post topic-related, intriguing pictures, icons, phrases, quotations, charts, etc., on the walls around the room. Tape a welcome sign on the door. These posters provide a preview of what is to come.

FOOTPRINTS. Create interest by cutting out colorful "footprints" and have them walking into your meeting room. 🔎

CLUTTER. Get rid of the clutter that tends to build up in a meeting room, especially at the front where you will be doing most of your speaking. What kind of clutter? Empty water glasses, piles of materials left over from a previous session, furniture that serves no purpose. Need I go on? Physical clutter leads to mental clutter for both you and your audience.

Try this out during the next presentation you attend. Look at the area around the speaker and the audience members. Notice the clutter that doesn't serve the presentation and could be removed easily.

PREPARE YOUR HANDOUTS, WORKBOOKS, OR TAKEAWAYS ⚠

The ultimate purpose of your handout, workbook, or takeaway should be to enhance your speech, not detract from you or your message. Inquiring minds want to know: what is the difference between the three? This should help:

- A *handout* is printed material that encapsulates the presentation. It can be in the form of an agenda, an outline, PowerPoint slide printouts, fact sheets, a list of references, a spreadsheet, or an article handed out prior to or during the presentation. It can also include promotional materials about you, your organization, or your product or service.
- A *workbook* is an extended handout typically used for training sessions.
- A *takeaway* can be the same thing as your handout or some other gift; the only difference is that it's given to attendees as they leave the meeting.

One reason handouts exist is so that the audience can take notes while you are speaking. When people write things down, they are also more likely to remember the salient points, even if they never go back and look at their notes again. Handouts also provide audience members with a sense of security, especially during highly technical presentations, because they know that detailed information is there to refer to if necessary. As an added benefit to you, should your technology fail, you can always rely on your handouts.

Sounds like you should always have a handout, right? Not so fast; there are two sides to every coin. If you give the audience material to refer to while you talk, you run the risk of losing the attention of a large percentage of your audience. They will be looking at and reading the handout rather than listening to you. They will also be flipping ahead, trying to figure out what you *are going* to say rather than listening to what you *are* saying!

HAVE A HANDOUT STRATEGY

There is no "right" or "wrong" answer, but you do have choices when it comes to using handouts:

- Put the handouts on each chair or on the table at each place right before people come in.

INTERACTIVE TONE

- Distribute your handout as people walk in. The ushers at church do this quite efficiently.
- Distribute your handout at a specific moment during your presentation.
- Save your handout for the end of your speech. Now it's called a takeaway!
- Consider distributing your handout and any other supplemental information in PDF format on a flash drive or providing a Web page URL you encourage the audience to visit.

Figure out your strategy and tell the participants up front so they can know what to expect. Unless, of course, you want it to be a surprise!

DESIGN ENGAGING HANDOUTS

Why settle for boring handouts? Especially if you choose to distribute your handouts at the beginning, you want them to be visually engaging:

- Be creative. Use color, drawings, or other artwork where appropriate.
- Be a name-dropper. Put high-profile participants' names in the handout.
- Insert opportunities to "fill in the blank" as the session proceeds. Make sure you cover all the "blanks" because people will want to know what goes in them.
- Color code, number your key points and pages, or create icons for each segment so people can follow along.
- Clearly label your charts and diagrams so participants can quickly find the appropriate spot on your handout.
- Headline your key points with lots of white space so participants can take notes, or have a specific area designated for note taking. You can provide supplemental detail in your takeaway.
- Proofread your documents for clarity (is your message coming across clearly?), accuracy (there is always someone who will spot a typo!), and professional quality (are you proud of your handout?).

Bottom line: You should always give a handout *or* a takeaway that summarizes your main point(s) and provides your contact information if the audience has any further questions. Your materials subtly speak for you long after your presentation is done.

"THE MAGIC WORD—YOUR NAME!"

Joel Weldon, CPAE Speaker Hall of Fame

How do you design engaging handouts? Find out who knows your audience—a key player with the ability to give you the inside information about current issues, events, products, programs, and people you can "work into" your message and tie into your stories. One specific question would be "Who in your organization is known by at least 50 percent of the group and fits these descriptions?" (You can use one, two, or even three names for each if they fit in.)

♦ Long-time employees who love their job?

♦ Very enthusiastic and positive?

♦ Fit and works out regularly?

♦ Great at customer service?

Okay, you get the point. My list usually generates twenty-five to fifty names, and yes, each one is used in my presentation or in the printed materials.

Now for the custom handouts. We hired a young college student way back in 1980 to create custom artwork and cartoon characters for our handouts. Now, almost thirty years later, Brad Hall still does our cartoons. We have thousands of them to use in our handouts that represent the stories or situations I speak about. The handouts then have all the content of my verbal message and the customized comments about some of those twenty-five to fifty people.

Now it's your turn. Start off small and see if just one to two customized references to people give you the magic word your audiences love to hear—their own name!

Just ask Mary Lou Becker how she handles returns. She's amazing.
Her CSI rating keeps us number one in our customers' eyes.

PRESENTATION PACKING LIST

PRESENTER MATERIALS

- ☐ Props
- ☐ Gifts/prizes
- ☐ Prepared easel charts/posters
- ☐ Copy of introduction
- ☐ Noisemaker
- ☐ Costume

PARTICIPANT MATERIALS

- ☐ Response cards
- ☐ Handouts/guidebooks/takeaways
- ☐ Preprinted index cards with a provocative question
- ☐ Nametags/tents
- ☐ Scratch paper/pencils
- ☐ Sticky notes/index cards
- ☐ Instruction sheets

ROOM SET

- ☐ Sign on/by door
- ☐ Footprints on the floor
- ☐ Yellow police tape
- ☐ Easel charts
- ☐ Markers/pens
- ☐ Masking tape/stickpins
- ☐ Data projector
- ☐ External speakers
- ☐ Extension cords and cables
- ☐ Duct tape
- ☐ Working spare bulb
- ☐ Backup on a flash drive
- ☐ Music

OTHER

- ☐ _____
- ☐ _____
- ☐ _____

PACK EVERYTHING YOU NEED △

When it comes to interacting with your audience, you need to do more than show up. Be prepared to engage by having your bag of stuff—whatever that may be—at the ready.

As you create your presentation, create a checklist of what you'll need. When the day of the speech arrives, consult your checklist, assemble your stuff, and away you go!

OBSERVE AND MINGLE △

Believe it or not, you have an amazing opportunity to connect with your audience *even* as you travel to and set up the venue for your speech.

BE ACCESSIBLE. You just never know who is going to be in your audience or where you might encounter them. Some of them could be traveling on the same plane or others might be hanging out in the lobby. You want the buzz to be that you are a warm and engaging person. Even if it took you ten hours and five plane changes, be kind and gracious.

OBSERVE. When you get to the venue, observe the group's dynamics. If you can, attend the events and listen to the speakers who precede you. Depending on what is happening before your presentation, you may need to realign expectations. For example, I was speaking a few days after 9/11, and I had to reframe my opening comments to acknowledge the company's losses and the nation's pain and suffering. Hopefully, we won't have another 9/11, but be sensitive to the fact that your audience may be facing a calamity of their own.

MINGLE. Prior to your presentation, chat with as many friendly faces as you can. Casually listen in on their conversations to get a sense for the mood in the room. Introduce yourself. Shake people's hands. Thank them for coming. Get to know their names. Ask them easy questions, such as, "What's your name and where do you hail from?" or "What brings you here today?" or "What's your biggest challenge relating to . . .?"You are not only establishing rapport with the audience but also gathering valuable information *about*

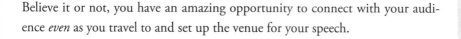

them that you can incorporate into your presentation. Then, during your speech, you can refer to them by name and repeat what they said. Just watch them puff up with pride when you mention their name!

- While you are mingling around, you can get a sense of who would be a good volunteer or whom you can ask to help with a specific task.

- Meet with the influencers, heavy hitters, and any of the experts on this topic so you can include them or defer a question to them.

- The extra side benefit is that mingling warms you up. Because you have spent some time with them, you will be speaking to friends rather than strangers. When you care, you speak with more passion and conviction.

ENGAGE AS THEY ENTER ⚠ ⚠

As the participants walk into the meeting room, send a clear signal that your presentation is going to be engaging and interactive.

MUSIC. Play upbeat, popular, age-appropriate music as attendees gather before your presentation, when you take the stage, or during breaks. Select songs that extend your theme into the meeting, and don't forget to license

the use of that piece of music! To obtain information, permission, and/or purchase rights to use music for a public performance, contact ASCAP (www.ascap.com) or BMI (www.bmi.com).

SLIDE SHOW. Create a slide show with interesting tidbits of information related to your topic, such as a quotation, an interesting fact, or trivia questions (like those used at a movie theater). You can also insert pertinent facts about yourself in order to establish your credibility. For example, when I speak about teamwork, I use a "looping" PowerPoint file of interesting team quotations called "Team Quotables." You can see a demonstration at www.TeamQuotables.com. 🔍

LIVE FEED. You have probably seen this technique at concerts and sporting events, where a stream of text messages is projected for all to see. You can do this too prior to any presentation through Twitter or other text messaging or chat room vehicles. 🔍

INDEX CARD. Rather than distributing a handout, place a 3 x 5 card at each seat. Pose an intriguing question and ask the audience to complete the card, or preprint the question on the card. For example, "What is your greatest business challenge right now?" Collect the cards and either quote some of the answers in your speech or collect the data and feed it back to the meeting organizer.

PROPS. Place colorful toys or other topic-related objects on the tables. It will certainly pique everyone's curiosity and may assist you in a group activity or in separating the audience into smaller groups. 🔍

IN MEDIAS RES. As people walk into the room, start them working on something either individually or together. For example, have them create a list, craft a definition, or solve a puzzle. As people continue to enter the room, encourage them to join in the activity.

The goal here is to do things that send the message that you have prepared for this presentation and the audience is in good hands. They will expect that something different is going to happen in your meeting. They should be bored no more.

START SMARTLY ⚠ ⚠

It's showtime! Either you are formally introduced or you kick off the session without much ado. Take a deep breath and establish a connection between you and the participants at the very beginning. Involve them right from the start with a low-risk technique. As they get to know you and trust you, you can try some higher-risk techniques.

INTERACTIVE TONE

FORMAL INTRODUCTION. A formal introduction should create a connection between you and your audience as well as establish your expertise on the topic. Rather than ask some reputable person to read your entire bio or to wing it, carve out the few snippets your audience truly cares about—either information that enhances your credibility in their eyes or is a common trait that connects you to your audience. Give the introducer a suggested intro printed in a large font (at least 16-point), and ask him or her to read it with vigor.

If you have time, and the introducer is willing to practice your intro or be coached through it, you may want to infuse your introduction with one of the techniques in this book as well.

ENTER STAGE RIGHT. Since we read left to right, walk up to the front of the room from the left side of the room. Similarly, when you finish, exit stage left.

HANDSHAKE. Don't forget to genuinely shake the hand of the person who introduces you. It conveys a simple image of connection that resonates out into the audience. If appropriate, make a kind, positive comment about the introducer. Since most of the people in the room already know the introducer, they become a tad bit more comfortable with you because of the collegial association.

CONNECT. You have one to two minutes to solidify your connection with the participants. While every audience has a different personality, they all want to know that they are in good hands; they need to know you care about them and they can trust you. Depending on your comfort level, select a technique from this book and adjust it to work with your topic. Following are several specific connection techniques that you could use at the very beginning of your presentation:

• Ask participants a provocative question about their top issues, ideas, and thoughts about the topic.

- Share something interesting and complimentary based on what you have discovered about them. Everyone is always eager to hear about themselves and how they compare to others.

- Share the results of the survey you took earlier and how that compares to others.

- Create an icebreaker or game that ties to the topic.

- Share the impact (benefits as well as unfavorable consequences) of your topic on the reality of their lives if the present situation is/is not resolved.

- Take a meaningful poll to discover commonalities among the participants— where the answers are interesting to you as well as the audience.

- Offer a direct-to-the-heart-of-the-matter statement that links everyone in the room to your subject.

- Report a startling statistic that hooks them in.

- Pair participants up to share with each other something relatively quick and easy to answer.

- Share a recent occurrence or success story related to the topic.

- Ask the audience, on a scale of one to ten, how affected they are by the topic.

- Get the ball rolling with one of a gazillion conversation starters.

IT'S NOT ABOUT YOU. I know it's hard. I like to be center stage too. I always open with a story about myself, don't you? It is all about me, isn't it? (Note the satire?) It is very difficult to do, regardless of whether you are writing or giving a presentation, but try as best you can to stay away from making it all about you. And please, *please* do not start with an apology such as "Sorry for running late" or "My apologies for my slides how . . ." I hate to break this to you, but no one cares what your problems are. They care about what you are going to say that will make their lives better.

 Don't forget to check out more resources and downloads at www.boringtobravo.com.

CHAPTER TWO RECAP

What are some of the specific things you can do to set the tone for interaction?

- Reach out and connect with your audience.
- Grab 'em with a lively title.
- Build on the meeting theme.
- Make the room more engaging.
- Prepare your handout, workbook, or takeaway.
- Pack everything you need.
- Observe and mingle.
- Engage as they enter.
- Start smartly.

ACTION PLAN

Based on the information in this chapter, I intend to

Continue _____

Start _____

Stop _____

CHAPTER THREE
YOU ARE THE NUMBER ONE VISUAL

IN THE EARLY DAYS of staged performances when there was no electricity, the light on the performer was cast by burning chalky lime in pots at the front of the stage. When performing downstage near the pots, you were considered to be in the limelight.

While we have electricity these days to power the lights, sound systems, and multimedia projectors, never forget that the audience is coming to hear *you*. You are the number one visual in any presentation. While you are in the limelight, your connection to the audience, your energy, and your message are more important than any other visuals you may use. If you don't agree, then just e-mail your visuals out to the list of attendees and skip the presentation!

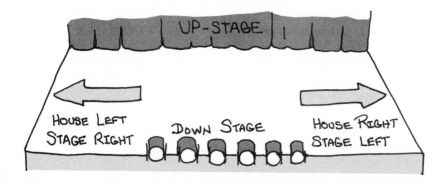

CONNECT WITH YOUR EYES ⚠

An English poet once said our eyes are a window to our soul. In our Western culture, we like to look people in the eye, and we trust those who reciprocate. If you truly want to connect with an audience, use your eyes to create a series of intimate mini-conversations with every person in the room.

ESTABLISH RAPPORT. Before you begin to speak, establish rapport with the audience by letting your eyes sweep the room: look from one side to the other and from front to back. Make eye contact with as many people as you can. Start a mini-conversation with your eyes to telegraph that you care about those you are presenting to and are glad to be among them. The participants will respond to your heartfelt "hello."

CONNECT WITH ONE. As you begin your talk, look at a friendly face in the audience and stay with that person for a sentence or two, or until you complete a thought. Allow yourself enough time to connect with that person—typically three to five seconds. You will actually sense the person's eyes responding to yours. Then move to someone else in the room, distributing your mini-conversations smoothly and deliberately throughout the room, without being too predictable as to where you will go next.

Most speakers have a natural tendency to favor one side of the room, so make sure you cover the room proportionally. The goal is to build a relationship with every single person in the room. Look at as many individuals as you can without dwelling on one person—such as the decision maker—in particular (We have all sat in on presentations given to the big boss; wasn't very engaging, was it?)

If you make eye contact with someone who quickly turns away, looks bored, or seems uninterested, move on to a friendly face. You will find that as you continue to connect with each person, even those who refused to make eye contact early in the presentation will eventually look interested.

If the room is really large, break the room up into quadrants and speak to one person at a time in different quadrants. The people in that section will think you are looking directly at them. Don't forget to play to the "cheap seats" in the far corners. If they feel included, then everyone will feel included.

PUNCTUATE WITH YOUR EYES. You can also use eye contact to punctuate an important point, make a challenging statement, or share an emotional perspective. For example, you can gaze into space when contemplating a rhetorical question. Laugh with your eyes when being humorous. Look askance when showing skepticism. After you have asked a question, open your eyes widely while raising your eyebrows to invite a response from the audience.

OBSERVE. Keenly watch for observable cues as you present. Are men and women smiling back at you? This is good news! Are they nodding their heads? Also good news, but don't mistake a head nod for agreement. It just means they are listening. Of course, nodding off is the ultimate sign of boredom (or someone just stayed up too late the night before, has jet lag, etc.). Yawning, checking cell phones, and fingernail picking are also pretty significant cues. When you see these kinds of behaviors from your audience, you must decide what to do about it: you can stay the course, probe further, or change it up with another technique from this book.

LOOK AT THE TIME. If you're lucky, a timepiece will be somewhere within your view: a clock on the wall, a timer at the lectern, your cell phone display, or the watch on your wrist. Don't worry about glancing at your watch every once in a while. It sends the signal that you want to stay on time, which people really appreciate. Going over your allotted time is a *huge* faux pas. No matter how much the audience adores you and what you are saying, do *not* go more than a few minutes over—*ever*!

#I VISUAL—YOU!

EXPERIMENT: MAKING EYE CONTACT

Practice making eye contact with yourself by staring into a mirror; time yourself to get a feel for how long three to five seconds is. Expand this practice to your friends and note how they react. Then expand your practice to people at work, on the street, in the supermarket, or other public places. Note how these people react to your eye contact, and then make changes as appropriate.

SMILES AND OTHER FACIAL EXPRESSIONS ⚠

Did you know that your face has more than twenty muscles that are capable of expressing at least four thousand different expressions? You have a wide range of facial gestures to draw upon to make your message more meaningful and more interesting to the listener.

The key to connecting with your audience is to make sure that your facial expression aligns with the message you are conveying—and is delivered just a tad before the emotion needs to register. For example, if you are going to tell a humorous story, precede it with a smile. If you are about to declare something as an absolute truth, a sterner look would be appropriate.

SMILE. For most presentations, you want to convey a positive, warm vibe, so keep a happy look on your face. Some people call this a "smile." Try smiling even before your speech; it will put in you in a positive mood. Before you begin to present, look out to your audience with a big smile. This will put your audience in a positive mood, too.

NOD. Periodically nod to a participant and you will notice that she will nod back, especially if you make eye contact with her at the same time. (Use this technique sparingly or you'll have the ping-pong effect!)

BE GENUINE. The key is to be authentic and genuine, allowing your natural facial expressions to shine through. Don't try to force yourself to be more animated. Just let your features reflect your natural enthusiasm and passion.

EXPERIMENT:
MIRROR, MIRROR ON THE WALL

To use facial expressions to engage your audience you must first be aware of your general countenance. Take a good look at yourself in the mirror and ask yourself these questions:

♦ In a state of relaxation, does my face look naturally happy?

- Do I have a natural smile on my face, that is, do the corners of my mouth turn up?

- Does my face show a range of expressions? In other words, do different parts of my face (eyebrows, eyes, cheeks, mouth) move when I talk?

- Make a few facial gestures the same way you would if you were talking to a friend: for example, smile, frown, laugh, look askance, and open your eyes wide while raising your eyebrows. Are these big and broad gestures?

If your answer to any or all of these questions is no, don't worry. It just means your natural facial expressions may be constrained. While perfectly normal in small, intimate conversations, the larger the audience, the larger your expressions should be. There may be some points within your speech where you want to make a special effort to be a little more dramatic with a big smile, open eyes, or even an exaggerated wink!

SPICE IT UP WITH VOCAL VARIETY

Variety is the spice of life, and so it is with your voice. Do you have a monotone, like you're from Kansas, or is your voice modulated, like you are from Colorado? Go ahead; say the word *Kansas*. It's flat—much like the state's prairies! Now say the word *Colorado*. Hear your voice go deep and then come back up? Which sounds more interesting?

Your audience will quickly fade while listening to a Kansas-style speaker. They will also quickly tire from a constant stream of rapid-fire high energy. (I call this person a "sip from a fire hose" presenter who just wants to hose you down with everything they know about the topic.) Your challenge is to strike just the right balance with your vocal intonation. The following are proven techniques to vary your voice.

> PITCH. A monotone has a constant pitch. Use a wide range of vocal tones from a very low, deep resonance (e.g., when you have something important to say) to a fever-pitch high note (e.g., when you are desperately excited).

(Side margin text: #1 VISUAL—YOU!)

TONE. Express your mood (or the words) through the tone in your voice. When happy, sound like you are happy! When concerned, sound concerned!

SPEED. All of us have a comfortable rate of speed at which we talk. Classic examples are teenager Rory Gilmore of *Gilmore Girls*, who talks exceptionally fast, in contrast to Southerner Forrest Gump, who draws out his sentences. Depending on the mood of the audience, how receptive they are to your message, and exactly what you are saying, you can adjust your tempo to keep it interesting.

VOLUME. Adjust the degree of loudness to create interest. Try leaning over to an audience member and whispering into the microphone, "Sally, this is just between you and me." When you do this, everyone else wants to hear the secret too.

DIFFERENT ROLES. As you are telling a story, reenact what people said in that situation. Change your tone, the volume, the speed, the pitch, and the accent to show the different characters in your story.

EXPERIMENT: CHANGE YOUR INTONATION

Listen to your outbound voice mail greeting on your home phone, work phone, or even cell phone. Try different techniques to "spice it up"—varying the pitch, tone, speed, and volume. After you have tried a few combinations, actually record it as your new greeting and notice the response you will get in return.

USE INVITING GESTURES ⚠

One of the first "professional speakers" I ever saw completely turned me off. She had scripted the entire presentation down to the last gratuitous gesture. It was as if her speech was on autopilot and she was just going through the motions.

Unlike this affected speaker's mannerisms, your gestures, just like your facial expressions, should be genuine, natural, and aligned with your words and key points. Concentrate on having an interesting conversation with the participants and your gestures will happen naturally.

There are also a few gestures you can *deliberately insert* into your presentation to describe, emphasize, or prompt the audience to action.

DESCRIBE. Describe an object or process by moving your hands to reinforce what you are saying. For example: when you describe something that is tall, extend your hand up high; if what you're describing is large, extend your arms out to both sides of your body; when you describe something that is itty-bitty, press your thumb and forefinger together.

ENUMERATE. Audiences love lists. They also like to be reminded of where you are in the list. Let them know by holding up the appropriate number of fingers.

EMPHASIZE. When you want to reinforce an important aspect, create a gesture to support and underscore the concept. Tim Gard, a drop-dead funny speaker, does a thumbs-up with both hands whenever he talks about something that is, from his perspective, good.

CHOP. If you feel strongly about an issue, your natural inclination is to point with your index finger with your fist closed. Don't do it! Pointing at the audience is akin to being scolded by your mother. If you must make a point, turn that "pointer" into a "chop" by fully extending all your fingers.

REACH OUT. A suggestive gesture invites the audience to participate with you or to accept your ideas. For example, when you want people to

DON'T POINT   CHOP

answer your question, put both arms out with your palms up as if you are receiving something from them. Conversely, when you have had enough or are finishing your point, put your hands down or palms together.

#I VISUAL-YOU!

MODEL. When you want the audience to follow your lead, use a prompting gesture to model the behavior you want. For example, when taking a poll, raise your hand to prompt the participants to raise their hand. You are modeling the behavior you expect.

PRACTICE. When going over your notes or rehearsing your presentation, also rehearse the gestures you'll use. When you feel a particular gesture is needed to illustrate a point, just do it and do it big! Where appropriate, insert a few deliberate gestures until they feel comfortable and natural.

ATTRACT—DON'T DISTRACT!

Knowing that you don't want to turn off your audiences, review this checklist in the days before your presentation to ensure that your gestures attract rather than distract your audience.

♦ Vary your gestures. Don't repeat the same motion too many times.

♦ Use gestures sparingly. Simple gestures work best. Too many gestures in one speech can be distracting.

♦ Make your gestures wide enough and big enough to include the entire audience.

♦ When making gestures that progress from left to right (e.g., a timeline), you want to mirror the movement from right to left, so the audience is seeing the progression from *their* left to right.

♦ Avoid "closed" gestures that separate you from the audience. These include crossing your arms over your chest, rubbing your eyes or nose, putting your hands on your hips, or the proverbial "I'm better and wiser than you" pose of putting your fingers together to make a steeple.

♦ Avoid distracting gestures that don't add anything to your message, as well as any distracting grooming behaviors, such as touching or scratching your face, head, ear, hair, and clothing.

Always get feedback from a trusted source because it is hard to catch yourself doing something that comes naturally but could, potentially, turn off your audience.

MOVE WITH A PURPOSE ⚠

Your audience is instinctively drawn to movement. To make your point even stronger, move from one part of the stage to another. Move toward someone to get her attention. You can even step into the audience to create a physical connection.

You do not want to pace back and forth (doesn't that just drive you crazy?), however, nor do you want to stand there like a lump on a log. When you move, move with purpose.

STAND UP. You can certainly give your presentation sitting down, but it automatically shifts the audience into a passive "listener" mode. Plus, it doesn't do much for your energy. Even when presenting to a small group, stand up straight and tall, with your shoulders up and back. Your energy and confidence will grab their attention, increasing the energy in the room.

SKIP THE LECTERN. Nothing says you have to stay behind the lectern—or even to have one at all. If you need a place for your notes, you can still stand *beside* the lectern and glance at your notes when necessary. If you can, haul that lectern away and remove any other furniture between you and the audience. By moving away from the lectern, you send a clear signal that you intend to engage the audience.

OPEN UP. Signal that you are getting more comfortable with the audience so they will be more comfortable with you. You can put your notes aside, take your glasses off, or move closer to them. Mark Sanborn, best-selling author of *The Fred Factor*, takes his coat off and rolls his sleeves up after a few minutes into his presentation. Mark emphasizes, "I do these things not as a 'gimmick' but because I truly am comfortable. It is a sincere and congruent signal to send to the audience that we are going to work." A warning to the women, however: you do not usually benefit from removing any clothes, even a jacket, in front of an audience. I'll leave it to you to figure out why!

GET CLOSER. If you must speak from a platform, lean forward slightly to get closer to the audience. Move toward the audience to make a strong point or to create a more intimate mood. State your point to a friendly face, then take at least two steps to one side of the platform and state your point to another friendly face. Walk over to the other side of the platform and repeat.

#1 VISUAL—YOU!

TRANSITION. Let the audience know that you are shifting from one point to another through your movements. Change what you have been doing. If you have been moving, stand still. Go over to the easel chart. Glance at your notes. (It's okay; you're in a transition.)

BE BIG. Make your movements BIG. Make your movements say something. The larger the audience, the larger your movements should be. Don't be wimpy and small here.

USE THE STAGE. Use different parts of the platform for different characters or perspectives in your speech. Actors call this "staging"; it allows the audience to follow you based on your location on the stage. For example, you can use center stage to deliver your main content. Move to the right when you tell stories, or go down to the left when you ask questions and engage in discussions with the audience.

TAKE AN ASIDE. When you deliberately go off your topic on a tangent indirectly related to the main theme, make it easier for the audience to follow you by taking two steps to your right (or left—but always go to the same spot when you go on a tangent). When you are done with your aside, don't forget to step back to the original spot and continue your presentation.

GO TO A SIDEBAR. A sidebar is a specific type of aside where you are stepping out of your main role and making a comment on what you just did, describing how you are feeling, or talking directly to the audience in a completely different way. Again, when you are done with your sidebar, don't forget to step back to the center and continue your presentation!

WALK IN. When you walk into the audience, you get closer to them, you connect with them, and it gives them permission to have fun and participate with you. Always have a reason for walking into the audience: for instance, you can sit in an empty chair for a moment, lean against a table for an intimate conversation, or stand next to a participant you intend to interview. Even though we all favor one side of the room over the other, make sure you circulate throughout the room rather than just concentrating on one side of the room. Finally, if they can't see you, they won't participate, so make sure the house lights are on when you walk into the audience.

ASK A QUESTION. Walk into the crowd to ask a question. Look out at the audience and wait for a reply. Then walk back to center stage without turning your back to the audience. Expand your conversation to include the entire room.

DON'T DISTRACT. As it is with gestures, too many uncontrolled movements can be distracting. Put the pointer, marker, or remote control down when you are not using it. Avoid tugging on, pulling, buttoning, or adjusting your clothing. If something in your wardrobe doesn't fit well, don't wear it.

When it comes to movement during your presentation, my advice is simple: don't sweat it. Let your excitement and energy about the topic ooze into your expressions and movement—naturally. The more you try to force a gesture or a movement, the more unnatural you become and your focus shifts from the audience to you.

TAKE ADVANTAGE OF THE SPACE

Victoria Labalme, CEO, Victoria Labalme Communications LLC

In delivering your presentation, consider the entire stage or space at the front of the room. Most speakers do one of three things: stand in one spot, roam aimlessly about, or pace along the edge of the platform like a caged animal. Consider all "quadrants," especially those off to the side and far away in the corners ("upstage left" and "upstage right"). If you are going to stand in one spot or walk back and forth in a line, make sure it is by design—not by default. Be creative. Look for opportunities.

As a bonus, consider "site specific" work. If there are unique items in your room (an extraordinary chandelier, a stage set with a gigantic photograph, peculiar plants, etc.), see if you can find a way to mention or weave these into your story or content. Audiences appreciate this because it makes your presentation come alive and shows that you are flexible, creative, and imaginative.

#1 VISUAL—YOU!

DRESS THE PART ⚠ ⚠ ⚠

You are the number one visual, and your appearance can engage the audience as well. You have undoubtedly read about, heard, or seen presenters who dressed for success—and those who did not. I won't bore you here with a laundry list of do's and don'ts, but suffice it to say that you need to wear clean and pressed well-fitting clothes that either match or are slightly classier than what your participants are wearing. And don't forget to polish your shoes!

Dressing appropriately helps to establish your credibility and trustworthiness, but it doesn't necessarily help you engage the audience—unless you do the unexpected. You can intentionally alter your appearance so that your audience is excited and surprised and remembers your message.

Think about your topic, the theme of the conference, or the host company's slogan. Is there some way you can "dress it (meaning you) up" to add a touch of flare and excitement to your presentations?

DON A COSTUME. Wear something that is connected to your theme: a flashy tie, a feathered hat, or a jacket to signify the times. Frank Kelly begins his keynotes with an example of the power of first impressions. "I wear a suit that's one size too large, have bad posture, and carry a piece of paper. I start, in a very monotonous voice, 'Um, yes. I'm here to talk to you about leaving a lasting impression.'" Just as the audience begins to fidget and feel uncomfortable, he changes his demeanor and takes off the ill-fitting suit to reveal a well-tailored one beneath.

DRESS UP. As part of the event invitation, ask the attendees to wear their favorite sports jersey, Hawaiian shirt, or a specific color. You can also ask just a few participants to come dressed for a "part" in your presentation.

Professional speaker and Internet marketer Tom Antion tells a story about doing a customer service talk for a pizza franchise. "I asked one of the senior managers to march into the meeting wearing a filthy doctor's lab coat with ketchup all over it (fake blood). I had another senior manager come in with a crisp, new lab coat. I asked a simple question: 'Which manager would you like operating on you?' Of course, all the junior managers yelled out that they wouldn't let either one of these people operate on them. Everyone was laughing and joking around, but the point was made. They must keep their employees looking clean and neat because nice customers won't want to be served by grungy food service workers."

PLAY A CHARACTER. The ultimate visual combines all these techniques together to become a "character" within your presentation. Although you don't need to dress up to use characters in your speech, it is helpful for the audience to follow along as you change characters by changing something about yourself: your facial expressions, a turn of the head, your voice, your position on the stage, or even your attire. When dramatizing a dialogue between two people, a slight turn of your head toward each character helps the audience follow and understand the conversation.

Don't forget to check out more resources and downloads at www.boringtobravo.com.

CHAPTER THREE RECAP

After reading this chapter, I hope you remember these phrases:

- Our eyes are the windows to our soul.
- Start a mini-conversation with your eyes.
- Smile!
- Be far more Colorado than Kansas.
- Sally, this is just between you and me.
- Reach out and use BIG gestures.
- Move with a purpose.
- Dress the part.

What is the most memorable phrase you recall from this chapter?

ACTION PLAN

Based on the information in this chapter, I intend to

Continue _____

Start _____

Stop _____

#I VISUAL—YOU!

ENGAGE WITH ENHANCING VISUALS

AN EFFECTIVE VISUAL vividly portrays an idea or emotion that connects the audience to your message. It stimulates their interest, clarifies your ideas, adds variety, and helps them remember the important points. A great visual helps the audience; you should not use it as a crutch to help yourself.

The challenge whenever you use a visual is to take the focus briefly off yourself, put it temporarily on the visual, and then quickly bring it back to you. So make sure every visual you present is a visual worth sharing.

Contrary to popular belief, PowerPoint is not your only option (despite its being the visual of choice for many boardroom presentations). You can tap into other types of visuals to enhance your message: among them are props, prizes, and easel charts, as well as visualization techniques to help the audience create their own visual.

SOME GENERAL PRINCIPLES

The number one mistake presenters make when using visuals is talking to the screen, chart, model, or other visual. If you want to create a relationship with the audience, you have to look at them rather than your beloved visual.

FOCUS ON THE AUDIENCE. Talk to the participants, not to the visual. Stand so that the visual is stage right. Practice this a few times—not just in your head, but physically practice using the visual. Do a practice run until you feel comfortable using the visual and any associated equipment.

BE RELEVANT. Any visual you use must be relevant and enhance your message. Otherwise, the audience will spend their time trying to figure out how the visual connects with your message.

BE IN SYNC. The visual should complement your spoken words and not be redundant. As you speak, the logic of the visual should be revealed to your audience. You should not have to explain its meaning in excruciating detail.

BE VISIBLE. Your audience should be able to see or read the visual within a few seconds—even those sitting in the back row. If not, try something different.

KEEP IT SIMPLE. The best visuals are simple and easy to understand. If the material is complex, or you want more impact, think about how you can do a gradual build: start with an easy-to-understand visual and work up to the more complex. You can also put more detail in a handout or takeaway.

AVOID CLUTTER. Remove anything in the line of sight of the participants that does not add value to your presentation.

CUSTOMIZE. For each visual, see if there is a simple way to customize it for your particular audience: the topic, the event, the theme, and the organization—including its logo, tagline, mission, vision, and goals. When you personalize your visuals, it shows you care about the audience and what's valuable to them.

FIRE WHEN READY. Show your visual only when you're ready to use it. Introduce the visual and then reveal it—or, for a hint of surprise, reveal the visual and then introduce it. Don't forget to put it out of sight when you have finished referring to it.

NEVER APOLOGIZE. Murphy's Law works overtime when it comes to presentations—especially, it seems, when it comes to visual aids. You should be prepared for whatever could go wrong. If you deal with the calamity in a calm, cool, and professional manner, your audience probably won't even notice or will just roll with you. An apology, on the other hand, says, "I'm not Hallmark cards; I didn't care enough about you to do my very best."

USE PROPS

A prop (derived from the theatrical term "property") is any object handled or used by an actor in a performance. Simply put, props bring your words to life. You can use props to strengthen your audience's ability to visualize, understand, accept, and remember an idea, concept, or theme during your presentation.

There are several different kinds of props you can use.

ENHANCERS. Remember show-and-tell from grade school? Enhancers add life and energy to what you are describing in your presentations. I was asked once to facilitate a series of public meetings about the introduction of a nonnative oyster into the Chesapeake Bay. During the sixth meeting, an oysterman brought in a farm-raised nonnative oyster—which no one in that room (including me) had ever seen. All the while we had been talking about the nonnative oyster, but once we actually saw the oyster, we understood just how much bigger it could grow than the native species could.

THEATRICALS. Actors use props to help the audience believe and follow what they are saying. You can too. For example, hold up the magazine you are quoting from, or use a telephone receiver to take an "incoming" call. Vince Poscente, an Olympic speed skier and peak performance strategist, simulates a downhill speed race while standing atop a simple chair! That is one presentation you *never* forget.

METAPHORS. Metaphorical props are used to make or reinforce your point. For example, show a Slinky to illustrate the need for flexibility, or a telescoping spyglass to show how the family of strategic, business, and operational plans all need to be integrated with each other. In our everyday,

ENHANCING VISUALS

informal conversation, we turn the objects immediately around us into impromptu metaphorical props when trying to describe an event. (e.g., "The stapler is the car going westbound and this cup is the office building . . .").

MODELS. A model is a representation (usually smaller) of an object, person, or concept. Although you cannot bring a Caterpillar bulldozer into your presentation, you can certainly bring a toy model bulldozer with you. Doctors often point to an organ model as they explain a physiological occurrence.

Eric Chester, an award-winning speaker and strategist for educating and employing the next generation, created a memorable model of the average person's lifetime using a contractor's measuring tape. He asked one member of the audience to hold one end, then asked a ten-year-old to hold the tape at ten feet. Eric then unwound the tape around the room up to our average life expectancy of eighty years—hence, eighty feet. He invited audience members of a variety of ages to come up and stand at the foot marker that was closest to their age so they could get a clear picture of where they were at present, where they had been, and where they were going.

SIGNATURE. A signature prop is a uniquely created visual designed to reinforce your message just for that specific speech or for that particular audience. For example, Amanda Gore, an award-winning speaker and expert in emotional intelligence, joy, and being connected, uses an "endorphin" little yellow finger puppet that reinforces her wildly interactive keynote presentation "Live Out Loud." Nobody else uses these endorphins quite the way Amanda does. This signature prop is unique to Amanda, so don't you even think about replicating, plagiarizing, or stealing her idea!

HOW TO USE A PROP

◆ Keep your prop hidden until you are ready to use it *unless* you want to keep it onstage to arouse the audience's curiosity.

◆ Ask the audience to agree with you on something.

◆ Get them to nod.

◆ Introduce the prop to the audience. Hold it in front of you; hold it high and hold it steady. Move it slowly so it can be seen from all parts of the room. Do *not* talk to the prop! Talk to the audience.

◆ Put it away or out of sight when you're done. Resist the temptation to pass it around, because the handoff from person to person and each person's close inspection will be very distracting.

REWARD YOUR AUDIENCE

Recognize and reward participants for their willingness to interact with you with a freebie that promotes you and your message. In order for rewards to work, they must meet the CAD test: they must connect, be authentic, and require that the audience do something.

- Connect. Your prize must relate to your topic, your organization, or your comments. Just giving a meaningless tchotchke to spice up your presentation is a waste of everyone's time. But if it serves a distinct purpose and helps the recipient, you are doing them a favor. Try giving a book that you recommended during your speech, a prop, a freebie, or a gift card.
- Authentic. Your comments and reward must be sincere. You must care about the person and what they did and tie that to what they will receive.
- Do. The recipient must have to *do* something to get the reward. For some audiences, it could even be a gift just for showing up!

ENHANCING VISUALS

There are several types of rewards you can use.

PRIZES. Reward audience participation with a prize to the first person who offers an answer or comment. The rest of the audience will be more willing to participate. Financial planners love to hand out 100 Grand bars (formerly known as $100,000 bars) and chocolate coins wrapped in gold foil called "doubloons." It doesn't have to be chocolate, but even adult professionals will be eager for a chance to earn an inexpensive but interesting prize.

INDUCEMENTS. Give something of value if the audience does something you requested. For example, you can ask audience members to each give you their business card in exchange for a tip sheet.

GIFTS. When you just want to thank them, a gift is given with no expectation of anything to be given in return. You can place your business card or a removable dot underneath several randomly selected seats before anyone is in the room. Sometime during the program, tell the audience that you have a gift for some lucky people and ask them to look for your business card or dot under their seats. When the winners find the business cards, ask them to come up front. Ask them an easy question and give them their gift no matter how they answer.

DOOR PRIZE. A drawing for a gift at the end of your presentation is used to reward attendance at the entire event. Place their business cards or registration forms in a container and ask a participant to draw a card. Since the point of the drawing is to reward attendance, don't forget to mention that the recipient must be present to win!

BE SPONTANEOUS WITH AN EASEL CHART ⚠

Best used in small, informal groups (but can also be used for specific scenarios with larger groups), the mighty easel chart can spontaneously engage your audience in real time. As a facilitator, I keep an easel chart in the room all the time as a way to document responses or to describe a phenomenon (usually some sort of model).

TITLE IT. Unless you are using only one easel chart, write a title on the top of the chart in big, capital letters so people know what the following information refers to.

WRITE IT DOWN. Capture your audience's comments to your provocative question. Participants love to see their words and thoughts written for all to see, so make sure you are capturing those ideas with some fidelity. Be careful to write down their words, not your own version of what they said. If you are going to paraphrase, make sure you summarize it first, get their agreement (usually through a head nod), and then write it down. If you don't get their agreement, ask again or reflect it out to the audience. There is always someone who does understand and can put it more simply.

DRAW. Sometimes, you should draw what is happening. Keep your drawings bold and simple. Dr. Sue Morter, an expert in user-friendly quantum physics and bioenergetics, draws a basic human form on an easel chart. She then builds on this basic drawing while discussing what happens to your body when toxins build up from unresolved thoughts, emotions, or lifestyle choices.

DO THE MATH. Sometimes, you might ask the audience to perform a bit of mathematics in their mind. For some audience members, this is difficult to do mentally and they need a bit of visual support. So do the math on an easel chart to support their thinking.

SET UP STATIONS. Print each of your key points on a separate easel chart and post the charts around the room. Much like the Catholic version of the Stations of the Cross you complete your discussion about the first topic and then move on to the second topic. For added suspense, "reveal" the chart as you start talking about it by taping another piece of paper over each of your prepared sheets or taping the bottom of the page to the top and then unfolding it during your presentation.

🔎 Don't forget to check out more resources and downloads at www.boringtobravo.com.

CHAPTER FOUR RECAP

Consider the following statements. Are they true or false?

1. The biggest mistake presenters make when using visuals is talking to the screen, chart, prop, or other visual.
2. When presenting a visual, the visual should be on your left.
3. A theatrical prop helps the audience to visualize what you are saying.
4. Feel free to copy any signature prop you see another speaker use.
5. A prize is a reward for behavior you want to reinforce during your presentation.
6. An easel chart is a fabulous tool to use for large, formal presentations.

ACTION PLAN

Based on the information in this chapter, I intend to

Continue _____

Start _____

Stop _____

Answers: 1.T 2.F 3.T 4.F 5.T 6.F

CHAPTER FIVE

USE POWERPOINT
WITH PURPOSE

HAVE YOU EVER had this happen to you? In preparing a corporate presentation, I opened up the standardized PowerPoint template and started to fill in the blanks. Slide 1: Today's Objective; Slide 2: Today's Agenda; and so on. As I was filling in the template, I realized that I really didn't want to follow this preordained path, nor did I think that PowerPoint added anything visually to what I had to say. So I scrapped the PowerPoint, designed a one-page handout, and delivered a fabulous presentation.

While PowerPoint (or Keynote for Apple aficionados) seems to be the visual of choice in corporate America, please don't feel that you *have* to use this software. I believe audiences appreciate a reprieve from stultifying PowerPoint presentations. Is there any other way to get your point across without using a slide? Dig deep here. When I analyzed my endnote (a closing presentation to a conference or convention), I realized I had only one matrix that could benefit from my using a slide. I opted to use an easel chart instead. For larger groups, I became a "human easel chart," extending my left arm to the side and then my right arm up to simulate the X and Y axes, creating the 2 x 2 matrix.

There are going to be times, however, when you don't have an option *or* you determine that a slide show presentation will enhance your message. For example, I use video clips when I am speaking about "Boring to Bravo." Do I have to? No, but I find it much more effective to show excellent examples of people presenting.

This chapter will zoom in on slide show best practices (*not* everything you need to know about PowerPoint) to help keep your audience engaged throughout your presentation.

Keep in mind one overarching guiding principle: When constructing your slides, go heavy on image, light on words. If you put up too many words, you are forcing audience members to a make choice between reading the slide or listening to you. The choice should be obvious.

And now for the legal warning: Everything—be it photos, text, video, drawings, charts, etc.—you insert in your slide show must be created solely by you, in the public domain, or used by permission.

USE A SPLASH PAGE, ICONS, AND HYPERLINKS ⚠ ⚠ ⚠

One of the biggest liabilities of a slide show presentation is that you are locked into a specific path. Once you proceed on that course, it is difficult to redirect it to fit the audiences' desires. Fortunately, you can create a "splash page" to give more control to and collaborate with the audience: 🔍

CREATE THE MAIN MENU. Perhaps there are five things you think you should cover, but you're not sure which item is more important to the audience or should be covered first. Why not let the audience decide where to start? Create a menu of topics that they may want to discuss.

CREATE ICONS. Rather than showing a bulleted list of topics, create "icons"—a small graphic or picture that represents a key point. If you have ever watched a DVD, you can see how icons represent different scenes or episodes from which viewers can choose where they want to start.

USE HYPERLINKS. Insert a hyperlink from the main menu or icon that takes you to a specific frame in your presentation or to another presentation altogether (just make sure you have the new presentation open or you will waste precious time).

HYPERLINK TO MORE DETAIL. Just in case someone asks for more detail, embed hyperlinks to additional visuals that can immediately provide it.

RETURN TO HOME. On each slide, have a button to click to return to the main menu.

INSERT DIGITAL PICTURES

Insert digital photos of a member of the audience or a group of them smiling and laughing. People love to see themselves, so take digital pictures on-site and insert them at appropriate points in the presentation to represent teamwork, leadership, or any other point you are trying to make. You can also access pictures beforehand by either asking participants for them or liberating them off Facebook, Flickr, or other websites.

FAMILY. You can also insert digital photos of your family. Children are universal; everyone either has a child or was a child. One or two pictures create a connection between you and your audience. But watch out for inserting too many. Then it looks like you're bragging.

HUMOROUS PICTURES. Mike McKinley, businessman and award-winning speaker, takes a digital camera with him wherever he goes. He has captured hundreds of signs, displays, and events that he weaves into his presentations to demonstrate a point in a humorous way.

BEFORE AND AFTER. Everybody loves to see a good makeover. There is a good reason why television shows such as *Extreme Makeover*, *What Not to Wear*, *The Biggest Loser*, etc., are so popular. People want to see the train wreck as well as what is possible. Show before and after photos to demonstrate the power of your message. Note: Your "after" might not be an actual photo because it doesn't exist yet. If that is the case, then take a picture or make a drawing of something that represents what that future could be.

BEFORE: BORING   AFTER: BRAVO!

STOCK PHOTOS. Insert an interesting picture of a key word you use rather than using the word itself on the slide, especially if the word has an emotional connotation. For example, if you are talking about a time of day, such as the early dawn; a particular season, such as a snowy winter; or a well-known location, such as New York City, a beautiful stock photo can instantaneously transport your audience to that place. No need to write the word on the slide; they should be able to understand the significance of the visual based on the words you use.

INSERT CARTOONS, SYMBOLS, AND DRAWINGS ⚠ ⚠

Cartoons add a dose of humor, especially to an otherwise dry subject. When projecting a cartoon, size it to fill the frame for a greater impact. You may have to resize the caption so all can read it.

You can find cartoons in places other than the "comics" section of your local newspaper. Look in the editorial section for starters. Several business and trade magazines have a cartoon section. Google "cartoon, topic," look under "images," and see what you find. Check out www.BoringToBravo.com for a list of reliable vendors. 🔎 You may have to pay a onetime fee, but then it is yours to use forever or for a predetermined period of time or number of uses.

CLIP ART. Unless it is absolutely perfect to convey a specific point in your presentation, stay away from generic clip art. This applies particularly to the Microsoft Clip Art Gallery, which everyone is familiar with. You can purchase clip art specifically tailored to your industry or audience. 🔎

SYMBOLS. Simple, colorful symbols reinforce your message and provide visual interest without the use of words. For example, a green dollar sign represents the concept of money, a red arrow pointed downward stands for decline, or a simple number indicates which point you are on. You can also use a unique symbol that is relevant to your program rather than a boring dot for a bullet point.

Dan Poynter, renowned author and speaker on publishing and parachuting, uses Wingding "book" 📖 bullets when he talks about book publishing and "airplane" ✈ bullets when he talks about parachuting. Ain't that cute?

EQUATIONS. Think back to your high school algebra class. Is there a mathematical equation that can express your concept? Think combinations of abbreviations and visuals such as PowerPoint − Light = Boring.

DRAWINGS. Sometimes, you just can't find that perfect cartoon or tailored clip art, but you have a good idea of what it is and what it should say. Why not draw it yourself? This can be tricky, because you don't want the drawing to look amateurish. Try sketching out the visual first and practice with it. You might change your mind before you get to the final presentation. If you need to make it look more professional, see if there is a graphic artist in your organization who can dress it up, or outsource it. 🔍

CAPTIONS. In every audience there will be people who forgot their glasses, people who are seated behind a large person who is blocking their view, or perhaps people who are illiterate, even in very successful audiences. Therefore, always read the caption, especially in cartoons so everybody can enjoy the joke.

Keep a file of cartoons, drawings, and symbols that strike your funny bone or are particularly effective. You never know when you might need to use one!

SIX STEPS TO USING CARTOONS

Ann Herrmann Nehdi, CEO of Herrmann International

The use of well-selected cartoons is one of the easiest ways to inject timely and appropriate humor into your presentations. I learned this technique from my father, Ned Herrmann, a pioneer on the study of the human brain in business and author of *Whole Brain Thinking*. He was an avid cartoon reader who perfected the art of cartoon selection and timing in presentations. From my own experience and his guidance, I have developed six steps to your successful use of cartoons so you can find the right cartoon to use at the right time:

1. Select an existing presentation (or a presentation you need to develop if you do not have an existing presentation to use) and list the key points. For example, for

POWERPOINT WITH PURPOSE

a presentation on How to Increase Team Creativity, key points might include team dynamics, value of diversity, meeting tools, brainstorming techniques, etc.

2. For each point, list key words and attributes that you wish to emphasize in your speech. For the example above, if I selected "value of diversity" the key words might include styles, differences, team conflict, etc.

3. Go online and search for your selected terms, and select the best cartoon.

4. Prior to purchase, review your preferred selections to make sure they are not offensive, are relevant to the presentation and your point, and are truly funny. When in doubt, I will ask another person for his or her opinion before making a decision.

5. Integrate your cartoon into your presentation, making sure the copyright information is clear and the image and caption are large enough to be legible by everyone in the audience.

6. Practice your delivery of the cartoon as part of your presentation. Occasionally, I will show the image first, to set up the cartoon, and then show the caption in a two-step process. Timing makes a difference, so you might want to try it one or two ways.

The best way to get started is to try it. Start with your next presentation and progressively develop your style and level of comfort. You will soon find that you will not want to do a presentation without a cartoon.

USE DISPLAY CHARTS

Only an accountant would love a spreadsheet, but I'm not even sure CPAs love them all that much either. What your audience will love is the story the numbers will tell them. So think about the story as you put your slide show together. Each slide should be more than a statement of fact. After all, if it is only informational, why don't you just e-mail the slide show and ask if there are any questions? Your presentation should bring your perspective about what the numbers mean to the participants—not just to you.

There are an unlimited number of ways to visually display your data. Here are some of the more popular techniques:

- Bar charts show comparisons of data.

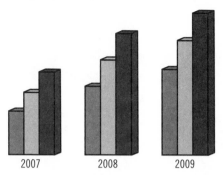

- Run charts show data over a defined period of time so you can see the emerging trends.

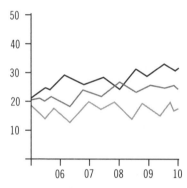

- Pie charts show the relationship of each wedge to the whole.

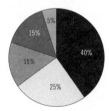

- Organization charts show the hierarchy and reporting relationships between entities.

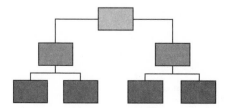

- Venn diagrams show common relationships between items.

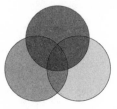

- Flow diagrams show an order, structure, or flow.

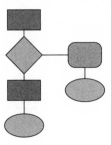

- Geometrical shapes represent concepts with three (triangle), four (square), etc., points.

Busy charts can distract the participant from the important point you are trying to make. Make your charts simple, readable, and clear. Now is the time to invoke the Keep It Simple, Silly (KISS) mantra!

Remember this word: "attribution." On the bottom of your slide, in teeny, tiny print, credit the source(s) and publication date of the information. This further enhances the credibility of the data. It is also required if the particular image or text is being used with permission.

EXPERIMENT: USE A VISUAL AID

The newspaper *USA Today* is the master of telling a story in just one visual. For the next week, check out the front page, bottom left graphic. What makes the visual appealing? What story does it tell? How can you integrate these techniques into your slides?

INSERT VIDEO SNIPPETS ⚠️ ⚠️

We live in a video culture. There used to be a few channels on television, and then MTV, VH1, and other cable channels proliferated. Now we have streaming video 24/7 on YouTube.com, Netflix.com, and Hulu.com, among others. As a culture, we are extremely comfortable watching TV and movies, and your audience expects no less from you. Don't fret, though: even a quick snippet of video that reinforces your message will entertain them. A minute or less is about right; otherwise, you may lose your audience. For example, I once saw a business speaker use a video clip of legendary golfer Tiger Woods chipping into the hole from the rough grass—and it barely dropped in—as a metaphor for hitting your goal against all odds. It took all of fifteen seconds and captivated the audience.

YOUTUBE.COM. A ton of engaging videos can be found at this site with the implied consent of the copyright holder to redistribute the video. That means you can reuse the video in your presentation—as long as it is still posted on the site. So check the site each time you plan to use the clip; the license terminates within a "commercially reasonable amount of time" once the work is removed from the website.

MOVIE CLIPS. Most audiences perk up when you use a short video clip from a popular movie. Again, be advised, when you use a video in a public meeting or training environment (regardless of whether you are profit or nonprofit), it is considered a public performance and requires the consent of the original copyright holder or its agent. To obtain information, permission, and/or purchase rights to use movie clips, contact Motion Picture Licensing Corporation (www.mplc.com) or Audio Cine Films Inc. (www.acf-film.com).

YOUR OWN. As you are doing research for your speech, take your video camera and film the audience in action at an earlier event and/or interview real people—the rising stars as well as customers. Show them at work, being successful. Splice the best of the best into one video or create segments to reinforce each major point of your speech. (So, you thought you could get rid of the lawyers this way, right? Wrong. If you plan on broadcasting your video to the larger world in a profit or not-for-profit environment, save yourself a headache and get each person's *written consent* to be in your video at the time you do the filming.) 🔍

PURCHASE CLIPS. You can purchase video clips that announce breaks, open or close a session, or provide a lighthearted moment. Typically, when you purchase the video, you also purchase the legal right to use it in a public setting. 🔍

CUSTOM VIDEO. Plenty of resources are available to customize video into your presentation. This gets a bit pricey, so practice due diligence and do a dry run of how you are going to use the clip(s) before you actually commission the production.

Improved technology makes it a lot easier to insert video directly into your slide show, seamlessly transitioning from one format to another, but only if you use your own computer. If you are going to use video, make sure you have the right plug-ins for your computer, suitable speakers so that people can hear, and a projector that can handle the video. If you are going to use video from another format (e.g., DVD), make sure it is queued up or have an audiovisual technician change out the formats for you.

Oh! And don't forget to move your mouse pointer off the slide!

USE COLOR APPROPRIATELY ⚠

A little bit of color can spruce up a dull, black-and-white visual, but don't overdo it. Using too much color is far worse than using too little. A general rule of thumb is no more than four colors per visual; otherwise, you will overwhelm your audience.

Color affects us emotionally through associations we have with nature, our culture, and our experiences with that color. You will want to use dark colors to connote authority, power, sophistication, and control. Bright, vibrant colors help keep people more attentive and are best used in small splashes to focus the audience's attention. Pastels are softer, more calming, and may even appear weak, so use carefully, if at all.

Generally speaking, certain colors evoke certain feelings that subliminally affect your audience's mood:

- Black is the absence of color and lacks emotional depth. Black is the color of choice for factual information in which the audience has no choice but to accept the data.

- Blue is a cool, conservative color. Strong blues instill trust, security, peace, intelligence, stability, and loyalty.

- Brown is an earth tone that conveys solidity and being grounded.

- Green is a restful color that represents growth, vitality, health, and life.

- Purple is a royal color that signifies vitality.

- Red is a "hot" color full of passion, energy, and fire. It also signifies danger, debt, and stop.

- Orange implies health and abundance.

- Yellow is bright, sunny, and cheerful and expresses light, optimism, and motivation.

- Gray is a neutral color that neither adds to nor detracts from other colors.

- White symbolizes purity, peace, cleanliness, and freshness.

You can also use color to emphasize, contrast, or differentiate one point from another. Though background templates add consistency to your presentation, they can also be boring. You can keep the template and change the color scheme for each major point. This will keep it visually stimulating while providing a bit of consistency.

When you add the visual component to your presentation, practice with different colors and get reactions from your friends and coworkers.

CHOOSING THE RIGHT COLORS

Dave Paradi, author of *The Visual Slide Revolution*

The most important aspect of choosing colors for your slides is to make sure that the colors have enough contrast. Contrast is a measure of how different two colors are, and it determines how easy it is to see one color when placed on top of the other color. When the text color does not contrast enough with the background color, the audience won't be able to easily see the text and thus won't be able to read it. The same issue occurs in selecting colors for elements in a graph or shapes in a diagram.

Most presenters, like myself, don't have a design background and can't just look at two colors and know if they have enough contrast. It isn't enough to look at the colors on your computer screen. Laptop and flat screen monitors are far brighter than projectors are, and as a result, they give you a distorted perception of how much contrast two colors have. How can you be certain, then, that the colors you choose will have enough contrast? Use the international standard tests for color contrast.

What are those? A number of years ago, the World Wide Web Consortium (W3C) created two tests that use the red, green, and blue (RGB) attributes of any two colors to determine if there is enough difference, or contrast, between them. They developed these tests to help Web developers create easily readable websites. We can use those standardized tests to make our slides readable.

I've made this easy for presenters by creating an online Color Contrast Calculator that allows you to test the difference between two colors you are considering for your slides. Just go to www.ColorContrastCalculator.com to use this tool. The page also contains detailed instructions on how to find the RGB attributes of a color and some ideas on what you can do to improve the contrast of two colors if they don't pass the tests. You can also use this tool as an objective viewpoint when discussing color choice with colleagues.

Two colors to avoid together if you can are red and green. Medical studies suggest that approximately one out of every ten Caucasian males has some degree of red-green color blindness. It affects each person differently, but men with red-green color blindness may see those colors as gray or faded, or they may not see them at all. It is better to avoid this potential issue by selecting colors other than red or green as the primary colors for your slides. 🔎

COUNTDOWN TIMERS ⚠

One of the biggest challenges for any speaker is to get the participants back in their seats after a break or small group interaction. Download or create your own countdown timer on the screen to keep your presentation on track. Audience members can easily see how much time remains and return to their seats as the last moments are ticking down. You can even include music in the slide show to add a flourish at the end.

Do an online search for "Powerpoint Countdown Timer" and you can see several different types of timers. Or you can download a generic fifteen-minute timer available on my website, www.BoringToBravo.com. You can then customize it for your audiences by adding the organization's logo, pictures of participants, memorable phrases, trivia questions, etc. 🔍

Of course, a countdown timer alone may still not get everybody refocused, but you can check out chapter 12 for more ideas.

MAKE SURE YOUR SLIDES ARE EASY ON THE EYES

I said it once and I'll say it again: When constructing your slides, go heavy on image, light on words. Here are a few other guidelines to help you create an engaging slide show:

POWERPOINT WITH PURPOSE

- Headlines only. Use eye-catching headlines or emotional words.

- Easy to read. Choose easy-to-read fonts in a point size big enough for even the guys in the back row to see. (Do a literal test: Sit in the back row. Can you read it? If not, then it's too small.)

- Number it. Put numbers on all your charts/slides. It is easier to go back to "slide 11" rather than that chart about numbers of widgets.

- Animation. Use animation sparingly, and when you animate objects, swipe from left to right.

- Blank screen. When you are not using the slide, either "blank out" the screen or insert a blank slide. Keep the focus on you, the speaker, not on a slide you are no longer speaking about.

- Manage the light. Keep the house lights up so people can see you and your slides, and be sure to stay out of the projection beam. (Check the lumens of the projector with the house lights up. Can someone seated in the back row still read your slides? If not, dim the house lights, but make sure there is a spotlight on you.)

- Tape the light sources. Prior to your presentation, put tape on the floor to alert you when you are stepping out of the spotlight range as well as when you are stepping into the projection beam.

🔍 Don't forget to check out more resources and downloads at www.boringtobravo.com.

CHAPTER FIVE RECAP

If you choose to use PowerPoint, you are going to need to practice a bit more.

ACTION PLAN

Based on the information in this chapter, I intend to

Continue _____

Start _____

Stop _____

ASK ENGAGING QUESTIONS

A KEY SKILL for any presenter is to ask questions that stimulate the audience's thinking and get them involved. Questions enable you to continue the conversation, so set the tone for audience participation and collaboration by asking a few engaging questions early on in your presentation.

The key to asking engaging questions is to be thoughtful and deliberate. Keep in mind that you can turn off an audience with random, nonsensical queries.

When crafting an engaging question, be sure to consider the following points.

KNOW THY PURPOSE. Know why you are asking the question: to create discussion, to introduce controversy, to elicit a response or opinion, to review information, to provide insight, to determine their level of understanding, and so forth.

BE MEANINGFUL. Make sure your questions are meaningful to your audience, not just to you. Get rid of the truly stupid or patronizing questions that insult rather than inspire the audience (e.g., "Who here would like to be rich?" or "How many of you have children, or have ever been a child?"). When the answer is patently obvious, you have no business asking them such a trite question. Tee up something meaningful about your topic that will elicit diversity of thought in the room.

KEEP 'EM GUESSING. Your audience doesn't know whether you expect an answer from them until your presentation continues. You can ask the question and answer it, or you can address a question to an individual, or you can poll the larger group. Don't rely on one questioning technique.

HAVE TWO RIGHT ANSWERS. Don't put the audience in the awkward position of knowing that you have a "right" answer in mind. It just isn't fair—unless you are giving them a quiz. If your purpose is to advance the dialogue, craft your question carefully so there isn't a right or a wrong answer. Think through the possible answers so that you are comfortable with wherever the conversation needs to go.

SUFFER THE SILENCE. After you ask a question, pause a moment. Let the participants think. Then answer.

ADD VARIETY. Use various questioning styles and techniques in your presentation rather than boring your audience with just one or two techniques.

The rest of this chapter will focus on helping you add variety with various questioning techniques.

ASK AN OPEN-ENDED QUESTION ⚠️ ⚠️

Want to get the conversation started? Use an open-ended question—that is, one whose answer requires a sentence, not just a word or two. Open-ended questions usually start with the 5Ws and an H: Who, what, where, when, why, and how. A well-crafted open-ended question literally opens up the conversation space and encourages interaction with you.

Open-ended questions are like a tennis game. You serve one up and an answer comes back. Then you ask another, more specific question, and another, more specific answer comes back. As you volley back and forth with different participants, you'll move from general open-ended questions to more specific ones.

Make the question itself interesting. For example, you could ask, "What do you want to know?" or you could ask, "What is your one burning question you want answered today?" Which question do you think is more engaging?

Reserve the use of closed questions (i.e., those that have a yes/no or single word answer) to reinforce or punctuate a point in your presentation or to close the conversation and move on to the next point in your speech. (Just take a look at the paragraph immediately above for an effective use of an open-ended question followed by a closed question!) If you are going to use a closed question to introduce a point, set up the question so that you are ready to elaborate on it regardless of whether the answer is a "yes" or a "no."

Asking good questions is a skill to be acquired. Ask any teenager an open-ended question and they can clam up with a closed answer. Or ask any windbag a closed question and they can talk for hours. If you are not getting the response you are looking for, ask a different question. Keep the conversation flowing.

EXPERIMENT: ASK A GOOD QUESTION

Try *not* to think about this open-ended question: "What have you found most interesting in this book so far?" Didn't you find it difficult not to respond? Even if I don't like your answer, I have engaged you in a dialogue.

ASK A SITUATIONAL QUESTION

When you ask a situational question, you are asking the participants about their own experiences that are directly related to the content of your presentation. This type of question helps them recall or envision a time when they have been in a similar situation.

- Have you ever had . . . ?
- Did you ever find . . . ?
- How many times have you . . . ?
- When is the last time you . . . ?
- Do you sometimes . . . ?
- Have any of you tried to do [this]?
- Have you ever wondered . . . ?
- Remember how you felt when . . . ?
- Has [this] ever happened to you?

- Did you read/hear today about . . . ?
- Do you remember a time when you . . . ?
- If [this] happened, what would you do?

Situational questions are usually used to introduce the problem your presentation will solve or the goal to be achieved. Also, did you notice the word "you" is in every question? "You" is the focal point to a situational question because you are extending the situation beyond your experience into the audience's experience. It challenges the listeners to open up their file drawer of memories, flip through their current experiences so they can connect, and file the new information you will share with them.

ASK A PROVOCATIVE QUESTION ⚠ ⚠ ⚠

There is a momentous scene in the movie *Mona Lisa Smile* when Julia Roberts is teaching her first art history class at the conservative, Ivy League Wellesley Women's College in 1953. The house lights are off in a cavernous classroom when an enormous slide projector displays the first of what appears to be a progression of slides. The teacher asks, "Can anyone tell me what this is?" and one of the preppy girls promptly responds, "Wounded Bison, Altamira, Spain, about 15,000 BC." Another primitive drawing goes up and a different girl chimes in with the correct answer. The tempo of the answers increases, and we get the idea that the teacher doesn't have anything new to offer these students. We assume the teacher is devastated.

In the next sequence Roberts shows her students a curious painting they have never seen before. She lets them squirm and then asks a provocative question: "Is it any good?" Instead of spitting out a correct answer, her rote students have been challenged to *think* about what makes something art, and so the dialogue begins to flow.

When you ask a provocative question, you are encouraging the audience to think deeper about your topic. Some ways to create provocative questions include

- Take a key word from your presentation and ask the group to define it. ("We're talking about 'disruptive' technologies. What does 'disruptive' really mean to you?")

- Challenge the audience's assumptions. ("What do you know to be absolutely true about this topic?")
- Identify barriers. ("What will get in the way of our success?")
- Walk in another's shoes. ("How would your CEO answer that question?")
- Reflect the mood. ("What about this topic makes you angry?")
- Prioritize. ("What is the number one thing we should discuss today?")
- Provoke. ("What would it take for you to say yes to this proposal?")

The best provocative questions tap into the audience's knowledge of as well as their internal beliefs about your topic. So the risk is not so much in asking the question as it is in dealing with each participant's response.

HOW TO USE QUESTIONS TO DRIVE THE AGENDA

Having the audience drive the agenda is not for the faint of heart. You must truly have an engaging mind-set (see chapter 1) and the courage to go with the flow, to stray from your "script" and brave the rapids. Of course, you can quell your fears by thinking through the possible answers and figuring out how you can weave participants' answers into your presentation.

1. Ask an intriguing or provocative question, such as, "What is the biggest challenge you are facing in your business today?" You can respond to the first answer and that becomes your point number one. Reach out and ask for another answer to your question and that response becomes point number two, and so forth.

2. Make a list. You can simply listen to the ideas the group generates and make a mental list, or you can write their ideas on an easel chart or type them into the computer if you are really talented. When you write the ideas down, you can step back, look at the list, and circle the most pervasive items. Tell the audience your list and start with the most obvious and work your way through your list.

3. Summarize. You can take the top three themes that emerge and start with the first theme as your first point, the second theme as your second point, and so on.

ASK A RHETORICAL QUESTION

When you ask a rhetorical question, you do not expect a direct response from the audience; however, you do expect them to answer it in their heads. Many speakers (and audiences) confuse a rhetorical question with the technique of taking a poll, in which you expect them to give you a response to your closed question.

Phrase your rhetorical question for maximum impact by emphasizing key words you want the group to consider. After you pose the question, suffer a few seconds of silence. Patiently and calmly give all attendees enough time to collect their thoughts and answer the question in their own minds. Then, answer the question.

This technique is a favorite among many speakers; however, you can spoil the effect by asking the obvious question or rushing in to answer your own question too quickly, without giving your audience a chance to think about their own answers. Even worse, you could ask a barrage of meaningless rhetorical questions—one right after another—with the result that participants will simply disengage from the monotony.

TAKE A POLL

When you take a poll or an on-the-spot quick survey or quiz, you are expecting the audience to respond to your question en masse.

It makes sense to take a poll if you really want to know the information *and* if you are in a room where you can see the participants. (Sometimes the house lights are turned down so low you may not be able to see the results of your poll, so this technique won't work well.)

When presenting to off-site locations, think through how you are going to get their feedback, either through using the conferencing technology or by calling them out. I like to create a sign or picture of the remote locations or specific participants, just so I can remember to call on them!

Especially during technical presentations to left-brained engineers, lawyers, and physicians, take a poll periodically throughout your presentation to stimulate discussion and showcase the diversity of thought within the audience.

You can poll the audience through a number of ways:

- Round-robin. Go around the room and ask each person to state his or her position.

- Show of hands. Ask those who agree with your question to raise their hands.

- Thumbs. Have those who agree with the point you just made show you a thumbs-up and those who don't a thumbs-down. A sideways thumb can mean "undecided."

- Stand up. Ask those in agreement or who find the statement to be true to stand up. Those who find your statement to be false can remain seated.

- Noise. Clap to agree and stomp to disagree. Or, if confidentiality is important, ask those who agree to hum. You'll find those who are passionate will hum loudly!

- Shout. Say "Of course!" if you agree and "No way!" if you don't. The volume can also show the strength of the person's commitment.

- Response cards. Ask participants to select and hold up the appropriate color-coded card/paper that signifies their response. These are ideal for multiple-choice and true-false questions or those with a range of responses (agree/neutral/disagree; high/medium/low). (See the caution about color in chapter 5.)

- Continuum. Have one side of the room take one stance (definitely) and the other side the polar opposite (no way!), or think of your own clever scale ("vested" to "don't care").

HOW TO TAKE A POLL

♦ Ask the question and model the behavior you want. For example, "Who here . . ." and while you are asking the question, raise your hand high in the air. This sends a clear signal that you are expecting those people who can say yes will raise their hand with you.

♦ Suffer the silence while people decide and move.

♦ Report the result. You are the one person in the room who can see all the results, and inquiring minds want to know. Share the results in the form of a statistic: "That looks like thirty folks, so that's 10 percent of the group." (Want to make it a tad bit funny? Report out the numbers in a precise way, even though it is obviously a best guesstimate. For example, you could say, "27 folks agree, and that is 13.3 percent of the group."

♦ You can also zoom in on a couple of people near you and ask them some more questions.

Hint: Do a dry run, especially if you are using response cards or an electronic polling technique.

USING TECHNOLOGY ⚠ ⚠ ⚠ ⚠

I was listening to a presentation to seventy-five people not so long ago when a cell phone went off. Everyone took their attention from the speaker to glance at their phone perched on their belt or buried in their purse. It is downright embarrassing for everybody. It will happen to you sometime, so keep a few throwaway lines to lighten the tension:

- If it's for me, tell them I'm busy.
- Go ahead, answer it; we'll wait.
- That's probably my mother calling to see if I met a nice girl/boy in Philadelphia.
- Domino's Pizza. You'd like a pepperoni and mushroom pizza?

Ever since the humble cell phone wiggled its way into the meeting room speakers have been admonishing their audiences to turn off their cell phones. However, you can encourage the opposite and embrace the use of cell phones and laptops. Ninety-nine percent of your audience members already have a cell phone in hand, so why not use it to inspire audience interaction? There are some evolving technologies where you can pose a question to the audience and they can reply via SMS text messaging on a cell phone or their laptops. 🔎

You can also ask everyone to tweet. Just let them know where to aim their comments (your cell phone, Twitter, or some other online medium), and let it go. Admittedly, it is tough to look out into an audience and see a few people with their heads down, looking at their devices. Get over it. Assume they are taking copious notes or twittering great things about your presentation. Another side benefit is that the conversation is then magnified *outside* of the venue as other people can tap into it!

Dial it up another notch and you can use an audience response system (ARS). Such a system is typically built into your PowerPoint presentation, allowing the audience to select or dial in an option from a remote keypad. The software automatically tabulates the results and displays it in a chart, table, or other format for the presenter and the audience to view. If you choose to use an ARS, you will need to plan the questions (or at least most of them) in advance, and you will need to be extremely comfortable with the technology to make the experience seamless with your presentation. 🔎

ASK A SERIES OF "ENROLLING" QUESTIONS ⚠️ ⚠️ ⚠️

Close to the beginning of your presentation, you may want to ask a series of "enrolling" questions that tap into the audience's expectations or fears. It can also give you a focus in case you were not able to do an appropriate amount of exploration prior to the presentation.

When taking an informational survey, use the same techniques as for a poll, using the following preface: "Let's see by a show of hands/cards how all of you would answer the following questions." For example, if you wanted to explore their base of knowledge, you could phrase your questions this way:

- How many of you have heard of this topic?
- How many of you have some expertise in this area?
- How many of you think you should be up here giving this presentation?

Make your first question as inclusive as possible without being too basic or insulting, and limit yourself to three questions. No more. More than three, the audience will tire of raising their hand, stomping their feet, or waving a card at you. You can use the humorist's "Rule of Three" and make the last question a bit funny (see chapter 8).

ENCOURAGE ANSWERS FROM THE AUDIENCE ⚠ ⚠ ⚠

To continue the conversation with your audience you'll need them to respond to your questions. Encourage them to respond in several ways:

- They can just think about your question or comment. No verbal response is necessary with a rhetorical question.
- They can shout out an answer or freewheel.
- They can each answer in turn around the room.
- They can raise their hands and you select someone to answer.
- They can write it down on their handout or notepad for personal use.
- They can write it down on preprinted index cards or sticky notes.
- They can share their answer with a neighbor (dyad) or in groups of three (triad).

After you ask a great question, suffer the silence. Let the audience fill the space. Patiently and calmly give the audience time to collect their thoughts and the courage to raise their hands, shout out the answer, or write it down. Look as though you expect an answer, because you do. If you force yourself not to provide the answer, you will find that someone will *always* respond. Your audience will find the silence much more disturbing than you do.

Still nervous? By using a movement such as cupping your ear or putting both palms out, invite the group to shout out their answers You can even prod your audience by saying "Tell me!" Select and acknowledge a response in order to build a connection not only with the responder but also with the entire audience.

PARAPHRASE ANSWERS. Paraphrase or clarify someone's answer, especially if the entire room is not able to hear it. Create a headline; build on the answer and empathize with it.

ANCHOR HEADLINES. You may choose to validate several answers by writing them down on an easel chart. This anchors the comments and lets you return to them if necessary.

MAKE IT UNIVERSAL. Check with the rest of the room to understand and empathize with the responder. Ask, "Does anyone else have an experience similar to this?"

OPEN UP THE DIALOGUE. Challenge the group to add to the ideas and bring a fresh perspective by asking, "What do the rest of you think about what was said?" You can even be the contrarian to make the dialogue more lively.

ASK FOR EXAMPLES. Extend the response by asking for examples, explanations, or other opinions. Turn the Q&A into an experience that the entire room can share.

You can go the extra mile and create value that extends past your presentation by taking the results from the question (the easiest way to capture this information is from the easel chart or the index cards) and collate the data. Synthesize the results and send a copy to the meeting sponsor, meeting planner, and/or the participants. You can also write an article for the company newsletter, draft a "white paper" using the results, and even post the results on the company's or your own website.

INTERVIEW A PARTICIPANT

You are probably wondering, "Why would I want to interview anybody as part of my program?" Good question. A simple interview helps you connect with a single person in the audience. And because your audience knows that this part of your program cannot be totally rehearsed, you create a deeper sense of connection with everyone in the room—particularly if your interview is interesting.

Take Oprah, for instance. She has spent her entire career interviewing others, but we all feel connected to her as an individual. By watching her quiz, answer, ask, and respond to so many people, we not only learn about her guests, we grow closer and more connected to her too.

When you invite an audience member to be in the limelight with you, you are placing him in a highly vulnerable position. The person doesn't know what to expect—and neither does the audience! It is reality TV up close and personal. Unfortunately, your volunteer is not going to win a million dollars for participating, so it is imperative that you create a risk-free, comfortable climate for him. You never want to embarrass your audience volunteer and never pressure or coerce someone into participating. If, based on what you know of the group, you think you'll have to pressure someone to participate, either start with someone you have chosen and coached before your presentation or reconsider using this technique.

When interviewing an audience member, consider the following steps, which depend on your personality and style, your tolerance for risk, and your audience's history. If they aren't used to being called upon, you may need to increase their comfort zone before they can participate.

SELECT. Consider asking for a volunteer who is excited and energized to talk with you *or* preselecting a participant based on your prework. Be cautious in calling on people randomly, as that conjures up memories of being singled out at school when you weren't prepared.

MEET THEM. Go out into the audience to meet with them *or* ask them to come up front with you.

REASSURE THEM. Tell them that it's going to be okay, how great they are for volunteering, and that you are not going to make them look silly or do something stupid. Whisper reassurances in their ear or use positive body language that puts them at ease. You can even involve the audience by saying: "Isn't Sally doing great? It's so awesome that she has volunteered!" Be warned, however; if a person telegraphs her displeasure at being volunteered by someone else, ask a simple question and let her off the hook quickly.

ASK THE QUESTION. Ask an open-ended question that creates a connection or rapport with the person. Use his name first, and then ask the question. If you are using a microphone (preferably a cordless handheld one), don't let him grab it because he may take it as an invitation to talk a while longer.

BE IN THE MOMENT. Roll with the answers. Give the group positive feedback. Have fun, because if you're having fun they will too. After two or three more questions and some banter back and forth, ask a closed question to end the conversation.

THANK 'EM. Don't forget to thank each of your volunteers for participating and let them go back to their seat! Always be doing something with your interviewee; do *not* keep anyone standing on stage with nothing to do.

HOW TO INTERVIEW A PARTICIPANT WITH A TOUCH OF HUMOR

Brad Montgomery, CSP

Our audiences are craving an experience, not a speech. They don't want somebody to deliver a "one-man show" or monologue. They want a presenter who makes the speech feel like a dialogue. The interview technique lets the audience connect with you as a presenter and experience the session in a way that is interactive, fresh, and rewarding to them. And because they know that these parts of your presentation cannot be totally rehearsed, the connection we form with them is deeper. And the results can be funny. Sometimes hilariously funny. Got it? Connection first, funny second.

So how do we do it? Simple: ask good open-ended questions that cannot be answered with one word. You could ask, "What would you be doing if you weren't here?" Sometimes they will answer with something boring like, "Well, I'd just be on shift, making sales calls." That's not funny, but that's okay because at least you have interacted with the audience and are a tiny bit more connected. On the other hand, you might get an awesome answer such as, "I'd be home watching reruns of *Hogan's Heroes* and eating a bag of fried pork skins." Trust me, crazy and funny answers like this one happen more than you might guess, and the result is fantastic. This sort of answer would stop the program with laughter, and you didn't do a darned thing but ask an engaging question.

Another good one: "What is your secret passion?" You'll find that just by asking this question you'll often get a chuckle, partly because there is an element of innuendo to the query, and the answers you get will be priceless. You might get an honest answer, such as "I'm really into remote-controlled airplanes." In this case, you'd just follow up with: "No kidding, remote-controlled airplanes? That sounds so great. Well, I'm so glad you're here." Cool—you're a bit closer to your audience!

Or you might get something like, "Well, nothing I can tell you about," which will earn a laugh. If you're lucky, it'll get a huge laugh. Sometimes people will answer this "Have any passions?" question with just a simple no. That answer is a disaster, right? No! It's funny! Note that all three types of answer—serious, offbeat, or dead end—are great for you. You get a chance to connect—and maybe even get a laugh.

If you ask good questions, you will improve your program regardless of the answers.

WRONG ANSWERS AND OTHER MALADIES ⚠ ⚠ ⚠

Sometimes the answer is just plain wrong or completely off base. You need to be able to handle these "wrong" answers just as gracefully as you do a correct answer.

ACKNOWLEDGE THE EFFORT. Acknowledge incorrect answers with a positive response, such as "That's interesting. Let's come back to that in a minute" or "Thanks for sharing your perspective, Sally."

ADD TO. Add to the question with a subtle redirection by saying, "Let me add to that . . ." or "There's another factor to consider when you are looking at . . ."

REFRAME. Reframe the question and disperse the question to include others. "Let's take a look at this from a different perspective . . ."

RECAP. When recapping the discussion, you can summarize the fact that there are a lot of opinions about the subject. Then explain the correct answer in detail.

ARGUMENTATIVE PEOPLE

Argumentative people aren't looking for an answer. They are looking for recognition. When you have an argumentative person in your audience, stay calm, cool, and collected. Recognize their expertise, but don't let them take over your presentation!

- Allow them to say their piece.

- Paraphrase their issue, reflecting the meaning and voicing the feeling you heard from them. "I sense you are quite passionate about your position . . ."

- If necessary, ask probing questions to get to the real issue.

- Don't get hooked. You don't have to tell them everything you know on the subject. Answer the question as best you can in a few sentences. If the rest of the room appears completely enthralled with the question, perhaps you can continue. If not, answer in a way that connects the question to the objective of your presentation.

- Suggest you get together later to continue the discussion. Finish by saying something along the lines of "Sally, you have asked an excellent question that will take longer than we have here to answer. How about we meet later or after the program and we can continue this conversation?" Then break eye contact and move to the next question.

QUESTIONS FROM THE FAR SIDE

If you get a question that doesn't relate to your topic, you have a couple of options for dealing with it:

- Answer the question briefly.

- Artfully tie the seemingly irrelevant question back to your topic.

- Ask, "Does anyone else here have a similar concern?" If the audience doesn't, answer the question very briefly and offer to speak with the participant after the presentation. If the audience does, well, then go where the audience wants to go!

- If the question is really wacko, just say, "That is not what we are here to discuss" and move on. Your audience will silently thank you.

LONG-WINDED ANSWERS

When a question becomes a long-winded speech, you must politely yet firmly interrupt the questioner and ask him to "ask the question, in the interest of saving time." Your audience will appreciate your ability to bring focus to the discussion.

If you have trouble with this, listen to National Public Radio's program *Talk of the Nation* or other talk shows to learn how serious professionals skillfully focus the discussion.

Bottom line: Be polite, calm, and courteous. Answer as best you can, balancing the time allotted, the personalities in the room, and your objectives.

 Don't forget to check out more resources and downloads at www.boringtobravo.com.

CHAPTER SIX RECAP

Let's recap this chapter using a wide range of questioning techniques:

- Open-ended question: What is the most compelling insight you had while reading this chapter?

- Situational question: During a presentation, have you ever been called on by a presenter when you didn't feel prepared?

- Provocative question: What is the biggest concern you have about asking questions of the audience?

  _____

- Rhetorical question: You don't really expect an answer to a rhetorical question, do you?

  _____

- Take a poll: Have you ever confused your audience by asking a rhetorical question when you really were taking a poll, or vice versa?

  _____

- Ask a series of enrolling questions: Do you currently ask questions during your presentations? Do they inspire conversation with the audience? Once they get talking, do you find you can't keep up with the energy in the room?

  _____

- Encourage questions: How do you encourage questions from the audience?

  _____

- Interview a participant: How and when are you going to interview a participant in your next presentation?

  _____

- Closed question: Are you ready to move on to the next chapter on questions and answers, otherwise known as Q&A?

  _____

ACTION PLAN

Based on the information in this chapter, I intend to

Continue _____

Start _____

Stop _____

Q&A

I ONCE WATCHED a famous retired football coach deliver an after-dinner speech to a group of a hundred managers. As to be expected, when he came to the end of his presentation, he asked if anyone had any questions. What I did *not* expect is that no one had a question. Not one. Here is a guy with several Super Bowl rings on his fingers and no one had a question about anything he said. We looked around at each other for a few terrible moments until one of the VPs broke the ice with some lame question. There was another polite one and then the crowd started asking pertinent questions.

This question-and-answer session (Q&A) did not have to be so painful. Obviously, this coach had given this speech once or twice before, and yet his ending Q&A was the *first* time he engaged the audience one-on-one. Even though we knew what to expect, it is hard to involve the audience seven-eighths of the way into a presentation!

There is no law that says you have to save your Q&A until the end of your presentation. You can

- Take questions as you go.
- Stop periodically and ask for questions—particularly if a participant or two looks puzzled.

- Create small groups to formulate the questions.
- Use a cellular phone, Web technology, or index cards to solicit questions.
- Hold questions until the end (but then wrap up with your final comments or story).

There is no right or wrong approach, although I have a strong bias against holding all questions to the end. By the time you get to the end, your audience will have forgotten the burning question they had twenty minutes earlier. They will be ready to take a break and grab another cup of coffee.

It all depends on your topic, your audience, and how much time you have. Just pick an approach, tell the audience how you will take questions, and then stick to it. You may want to ask the moderator (if you have one) to introduce the Q&A approach, to call on the questioners, and to intervene if it gets off track.

TAKE QUESTIONS AS YOU GO!

When given an option, most audiences want to be able to ask questions as they come up in your presentation. To manage impromptu questions well, you need to be extremely comfortable with your topic and outline. You will be interrupted, usually at the oddest moments and with an even odder question that may take you a bit off track. You will then have to jump back into the flow without losing your place or momentum. Furthermore, you will have to answer the question without giving away an upcoming portion of your presentation.

HOW TO USE SMS TEXT MESSAGING OR TWITTER DURING YOUR PRESENTATION

♦ Invite your audience to tweet during your presentation with the appropriate address or designation.

♦ Ask a friend, colleague, or volunteer to monitor the "back channel" of tweets or text messages. This person becomes the "ombudsman" for the audience and is allowed to interrupt the speaker if there are any questions or comments that need to be addressed.

♦ If you can't find someone to take on the ombudsman role, monitor the tweets or text messages through your phone. Take a "Twitter Break" every ten or fifteen minutes to check the back channel during a short activity or Q&A period.

♦ Be prepared to change course and adapt based on what you see in the back channel.

♦ Midpoint in the presentation, check in with the ombudsman and ask, "What's the buzz" or "What are people liking or not liking?" You can also ask if there are questions that need clarification.

♦ Ask a few Twitterers to step forward to share their tweets (both positive and negative) with the entire audience. (Be sure, though, to give the audience advance warning that you may do this!)

♦ If you are brave and know your content inside and out, display the back channel on a screen that everyone (including you) can see. While this can be visibly distracting for some, and others will submit asinine tweets (Hi Dad!), you can respond immediately to any issues that come up. As a precaution, explain how you will respond to the Twitter stream at the beginning of your presentation, and they will be more likely to use it responsibly.

♦ The extra added benefit is that your participants answer questions and add explanations, elaborate on what you said, and share useful links related to your content. This back channel is a great way for the audience members to connect with you and to each other. They may even search each other out during the break!

Q&A

STOP PERIODICALLY ⚠ ⚠

If you decide to stop periodically and ask for questions, ask the group to text, tweet, or jot questions down as you go along, telling them you will stop every [twenty] minutes or so to take their questions. And then stop every twenty minutes or so to take their questions or check out their texts. This seems obvious, but time flies when you are giving a speech.

CREATE SMALL GROUPS ⚠ ⚠ ⚠

Although we cover small groups in more detail in chapter 12, you can ask the participants to break into groups of three or four after your presentation and discuss questions such as these:

- What questions came to mind while I was talking?
- What area did you wish I had covered more clearly?
- What is the one question that would help the entire audience?

CAPTURE THE QUESTION

Bob Pike, CSP, CPAE Speaker Hall of Fame

When I first started presenting in the Asia Pacific area, I was told that participants would not ask questions and that asking them questions would put them on the spot because potentially they could lose face. This has never been a problem for me in over twenty years because I have always used a participant-centered approach to presenting. I believe that the purpose of a question is for learning to take place, not testing to take place.

My participants are almost always placed in groups of five to seven, generally around round tables with the front (the part of the table closest to the visuals) left open. Periodically, I'll ask the group to come up with one to two questions they'd like to ask about anything I've touched on up to that point. I then give the tables one or two minutes to discuss and generate possible questions. Then I'll say that we have twelve minutes for Q&A and ask which table would like to ask the first question.

There is always a flood of hands. I'll take the first one I see, answer the question, and then ask that table to choose the next table to ask a question. At the end of twelve minutes, I'll invite them to post any other burning questions on a chart that I title "Capture the Question." I provide Post-it notes on each table for this purpose.

When asking questions, I will pose the question and then say, "Your group has one minute to discuss the question and come up with an answer." If it is something I have not touched on yet, I will say, "Your group has one minute to come up with your best guess."

STARTING YOUR Q&A SESSION

Depending on your comfort level, you can launch the Q&A directly out of the speech. When you take questions from the audience, step out from behind the lectern or take a step closer to your audience. Some presenters take questions while standing in the middle of the audience, allowing the speaker to roam and provide a personal touch (literally!).

Ask, "What questions do you have?" or "I welcome you asking me anything about this topic" rather than the typical opening: "Are there any questions?" Then pause and welcome their questions.

HAVE A BACKUP. If you find you are suffering the silence just a tad longer than you'd like, have a backup question ready: "A question I am usually asked is . . ." Integrate a question you heard from the audience either through your pre-program interviews or when mingling just before your presentation. "In preparing for this presentation, I interviewed some of your colleagues. One of the questions they had was . . ." This technique will often trigger additional questions from your audience. Follow up your answer by asking, "Who else has a question?"

LISTEN. When a person finally asks a question or makes a comment, listen to the entire question. Truly listen to what they are saying as well as what they are feeling. Look alert, maintain eye contact, lean forward, and stay interested.

Pay attention to your facial expressions and body language, especially with a naïve or difficult question. Try not to fast-forward to formulating your answer before somebody is done asking the question because you might miss some important information. Most questioners summarize their own question at the end, so listen to the entire question, especially the final sentence.

CREATE A QUEUE. If you are fortunate to have a number of people who raise their hands, start with the first person and establish a queue that lets the audience know who will go next. Then follow the queue. If you have a hard time remembering the order, write it down or enlist someone to help you keep track. Try to hear from everyone who has a question before you return to someone for a second turn. You can even offer that you are looking for new faces to chime in before you put a repeat questioner back in the queue.

COLLECT QUESTIONS ⚠ ⚠

In Q&A, you can answer just a few questions from a few people or ask the audience to "send" you their questions, sift through them, and answer those questions that are of the greatest interest to the audience.

As I mentioned at the beginning of this chapter, you can also collect questions using low-tech index cards, cellular phones, or Web technologies.

- Tee up technique. Give people the website or cell phone number where they can send their questions or distribute index cards.

- Ask for questions. Ask people to key in their questions or pass their index cards back to you or toward the center aisle and have a "helper" collect them.

- Sift. Scan through the list/cards rapidly.

- Select. Address the most universal and pertinent questions first. Leave specific cases for a more personal response later, if you so choose. You may even offer to be available to discuss the remaining questions right after the program is over.

- Collect. Go the extra step and create value that extends past your presentation. Collect that data/cards after the program, compile the information, and feed it back to the client or your audience.

USING INDEX CARDS DURING Q&A

Dr. Sivasailam Thiagarajan, better known simply as Thiagi

I often distribute index cards, asking everyone in the audience to write down one question a confused person might have about my presentation. Participants turn their cards written-side down and pass them to someone else, continuing to pass on the cards in a random fashion until I yell "Stop" after about fifteen seconds. I then select people at random to read aloud the question on their card—extending the option of pretending to read the question on the card while really asking their own!

RESPOND TO A QUESTION

When you are asked a question, treat each person and his or her inquiry as important. Respond professionally, showing that you truly listened to the participant and you desire to continue the conversation.

PARAPHRASE. Restate the question in another way so the questioner will know you understand it accurately. This also gives you a moment to formulate your response and lets you re-present the question for anyone who might not have heard it. Be careful of coming across as condescending or putting words in the questioner's mouth by using such phrasing as "What you mean is . . ." or "What you're trying to say is . . ."

REPEAT. If the questioner has summarized the question, repeat the end of his summary or pick out key words within the statement to use as your opening words. When you include this in your comments it gives a bit more credence to the question and the questioner, as well as your answer.

CLARIFY. If necessary, ask for clarification or probe deeper into the essence of the question. You can ask the person to define part of the question or give an example to illustrate the question.

PARSE IT OUT. You may find the question is really multiple questions in the guise of one. In which case, enumerate the different questions, and then answer them in the order that makes sense to you. You may even find the "question" is more of a statement, a suggestion, or an idea. If this is the case, acknowledge the contribution and don't even try to "answer" it!

BE NEUTRAL. Beware of complimenting the person or the question. Unless you are going to say "good question" to every single question (which will get rather tedious and might not always be true), other questioners will feel like their question wasn't as good.

AFFIRM. Although you don't want to compliment, you should be conscious of and acknowledge the underlying purpose or emotion of the other person's questions. Bring it out into the open with phrases such as, "I sense that this issue is very important to you. I appreciate you bringing this up."

BE OPEN. You may not like a particular question. It may be too basic, too obvious, or too technical. But it's not about you; your speech is all about meeting *your audience's* needs, so answer their questions as best you can.

SUFFER THE SILENCE. You don't have to answer the question immediately. Two seconds of silence to a presenter feels like an eternity. Two seconds of silence to the audience is a heartbeat and isn't even noticeable.

HAVE FUN. Let your sense of humor show (see chapter 8). Q&A is meant to be more informal and conversational, so lighten up a bit here. Avoid any note of sarcasm, criticism, or arrogance in your voice or choice of words, however; you don't want to offend a portion of the audience.

ANSWER THE QUESTION

You would think it's a simple activity to answer the question. In reality, you have six different options from which to choose or form a combination.

BE THE EXPERT. You can answer the question succinctly for the entire audience. Give the answer in one to three sentences or a full paragraph, tops. You have already given your speech; they don't need (or want) another speech! Choose what you say carefully, avoiding such controlling or overbearing words as "obviously," "always," "you should," "you must." Not sure how much to share? Tom Stoyan, an award-winning sales coach and speaker, simply asks the audience, "Would you like the thirty-second version or the three-minute answer?" He quickly gauges the audience's interest and responds appropriately.

BE THE FACILITATOR. Rather than answering the question directly, you can redirect the question to the entire group and ask for their ideas. This is a great technique to use, especially if you don't know the answer! But even if you know the answer, why not open it up to the larger group?

DEFER TO AN EXPERT. Where appropriate, call on acknowledged experts in the audience to share their views, insights, and impressions. During your prework, ask for their permission to redirect an appropriate question to them; you don't want to put them on the spot! *Always* take back control after they have responded.

RECOMMEND A RESOURCE. Especially if the answer requires a lengthy response, recommend a resource (website, book, article, expert) where the audience can find more information.

PARK IT. For questions that are important but are a bit off track or inconvenient to answer at that particular point in the program, you can ask the participant to write the question down so it can be addressed later. Or you can flip over a fresh piece of chart paper and write the question down on the "Parking Lot." Then, when you are ready to address the question, revisit the Parking Lot and answer it.

SAY "I DON'T KNOW." If you don't know the answer, and you don't think someone in the room can answer the question appropriately, do not fake it. Say you don't know. Offer to get the information and send it to the person, defer to an expert, or recommend a resource.

If you have been using PowerPoint during your presentation, consider putting the related slide up on the screen. Of course, that would require you to (1) number your presentation slides, (2) know the slide show order and number, and (3) know how to locate a specific slide. If the discussion is not related to any visual, remember to blank out the projection to eliminate any distractions.

At the end of the Q&A session, offer to answer any lingering questions by e-mail.

FINISH WITH A STRONG
CLOSING

If you must have a formal Q&A session, save a minute or two to wrap it up nicely. Always finish your presentation with a strong close: consider telling a story, making a memorable statement, recapping your main points, or inciting a call to action. Never, ever end with the answer to your last question. The audience will forget what your call to action is!

And don't forget to say "thank you," so that the audience knows that you are officially done.

🔎 Don't forget to check out more resources and downloads at www.boringtobravo.com.

....

CHAPTER SEVEN RECAP

Q. What are the five different approaches to conducting Q&A during my presentation?

A. There are five ways:

1. Take questions as you go.

2. Stop periodically and ask for questions.

3. Create small groups to formulate questions.

4. Use a cell phone, Web technology, or index cards to solicit questions.

5. Hold questions until the end.

Q. What is the biggest drawback to taking questions during the course of the presentation?

A. You must be extremely comfortable with your topic so you can adjust your presentation to meet the question and then jump back into the flow without losing your place or momentum.

Q. Why would I want to create small groups to ask questions?

A. Sometimes the audience may be too big to allow calling on individuals; you want to increase the energy in the room; or you want the audience to process your comments first and then ask more meaningful questions.

Q. What is the best way to start a traditional Q&A session?

A. Ask, "What questions do you have?" and have your own backup: "A question I am usually asked is . . ."

Q. What is the benefit of collecting questions versus answering them on the spot?

A. By collecting the questions first, you can sift through them and answer those that seem to have the greatest interest for the entire audience. *Plus*, you now have meaningful data that can be given back to the client and audience as a follow-up to your presentation.

Q. What if I don't know the answer to the question?

A. No problem. No one expects you to know everything, so you have a few options here. You can acknowledge that you don't know the answer and defer to an expert in the room. You can redirect the question to the entire room and get their ideas. You can also offer to research it and get back to the person or the entire audience.

Q. How do I finish the Q&A session?

A. Finish with a story, a memorable statement, a recap of your main points, or a stirring call to action and then a "thank you."

ACTION PLAN

Based on the information in this chapter, I intend to

Continue _____

Start _____

Stop _____

LET YOUR NATURAL HUMOR SHINE THROUGH

ONCE, A SEASONED SPEAKER was asked, "Is it necessary to use humor in a presentation?" The speaker responded, "Not unless you want to get paid."

I would take that one step further and add, "Not unless you want people to listen."

Except for the guy whose car you just rear-ended, everyone likes to laugh. When you make your audience laugh, they feel more connected not only to you but also to each other. Research has shown that we like to be around people who have a sense of humor. It's a human quality that breaks down tension and resistance and enhances communication and relationships. Plus, it makes the presentation more fun.

If you are naturally funny, then good for you! This chapter will reinforce what you already know. If you think you are funny but you really are not, keep reading; you may discover some valuable information in this chapter. And if you are like most people, who don't think they're funny at all, you will be surprised at how you too can succeed at creating a humorous experience for your audiences.

I am a person who has never considered herself to be funny. Humorists and comedians are funny. My brother is funny. Some of my friends are funny. But funny is not a quality I would use first to describe my presentation style.

But truth be told, some people find me witty, which brings a soft chortle, a gleam in the eye, and a smile to the lips. And I sometimes get a few chuckles from observational humor and stories that come from my own life experiences. I'm just not a laugh-every-six-minutes kind of speaker. But I have found ways of strategically using humor that can help even the most humor impaired among you (defined as those of you who never quite understood *The Far Side* cartoons).

In this chapter, I will show you how to let your natural sense of humor shine through during your presentations. I encourage you to stop trying to *be* funny and, instead, find ways to engage your audiences with a variety of humor that involves them. Before you know it, you may even be described as funny—in a good way.

A WORD ABOUT FINDING YOUR HUMOR COMFORT ZONE ⚠

The first principle of humor, and any material you use for that matter, is that it must be natural to your style and personality. David Letterman doesn't try to be Chris Rock. Chris Rock doesn't try to be Ellen DeGeneres. And Ellen DeGeneres doesn't try to be Joan Rivers. In fact, with all the plastic surgery, it appears that Joan Rivers isn't even trying to be Joan Rivers.

The point is that professional comedians are successful because they found their own style and voice. The same holds true for speakers. So, before you start to add humor to your presentations, consider these basic principles about finding your own natural style.

> **PAY ATTENTION.** What makes you laugh? Chances are, you will find out more about your own style by taking note of the things that make you laugh. The converse is also true. Don't pursue humor that you don't find funny.
>
> **USE HUMOR ROLE MODELS.** Perhaps you have a friend who is particularly funny. Or there is a humorist on TV, radio, or the Internet who

makes you giggle. Watch them for what they do and observe how they do it. See if there is something from their style that you can adapt to your own.

SEEK OUT HUMOR. Be a sponge. Read anthologies, collections of jokes for speakers, and other books on humor. ✎ Capture the techniques that work for you and adapt the material you like and that resonates with you. Just like anything else in life, the more you expose yourself to something, the more you will understand it and the more competent you will be in the execution of it.

KEEP TRACK OF THE HUMOR YOU FIND. No matter how funny something is, you won't remember it unless you write it down. When you find something that tickles your funny bone, write it down, clip it out, take a picture of it, or sketch with charcoal if that's your gift—and save it for future use. Create a system (a file, box, notebook) where you keep your found humor in one place to pull out just when you need it.

PRACTICE. Practice your bits of humor on a friend, your spouse, or your coworkers. If you're a member of a Rotary club, Toastmasters, or some other organization, take advantage of this readymade audience to try out your new ideas. If it works, you've got a keeper; if not, good that you found out before trying it during an important presentation!

BELIEVE! It's trite, but true. If you believe in your material, if you believe that it is funny, and if you believe that you can make others laugh, you will be more humorous.

NATURAL HUMOR

EXPERIMENT: HUMOR

A humorist friend of mine commits to trying out one funny piece of material at every meeting he attends. It is a challenge for him to come up with something, but it also allows him an opportunity to see how it plays in front of a live audience. Want to be more humorous? Set a goal: add one new amusing, witty, or entertaining bit every time you speak.

MAKING HUMOR WORK FOR YOU ⚠

Now that you have found your humor comfort zone, here are a few humor tips to make humor work specifically for you.

MAKE IT NATURAL. Take the time to understand and appreciate your own style of humor. Stay true to yourself, and don't try to imitate anyone else—and that includes Joan Rivers!

BE RELEVANT. Make sure your humor supports the content of the speech. There is nothing worse than irrelevant humor that distracts from the points of the presentation.

BE APPROPRIATE. Use humor that is appropriate for your audience, is suitable for the occasion, and is not offensive. While comedians often push the envelope with humor, a speaker's humor should engage, not irritate, the audience.

ALIGN THE AMOUNT OF HUMOR WITH THE TOPIC. If your topic is funny, then you will be expected to use a lot of humor. Otherwise, you need to spread your humor throughout so that it balances the serious material. After a presentation, you never want to hear, "That was funny, but where's the beef?"

GO WITH YOUR HUMOR STRENGTHS. If you can do foreign accents or funny dialogue, then characters might be your humorous strong suit. If you have a knack for telling funny stories, then weave away. Though variety is good, you should focus on your strengths.

SELF-DEPRECATE. You are not only the best target for humor but your humor is unlike anyone else's. By creating your own stories and using self-deprecating humor, you create a style of humor that will make you unique. Plus, it connects with audiences because it shows that you're not above laughing at yourself and thus are not above them. A little crack in the armor brings you down to earth and makes you more approachable to your audience.

You can use "you" as source of humor through the following means:

- Funny stories from your life in which you failed, screwed up, or stumbled
- Something obvious about your physical appearance
- Something you are terrible at doing
- Your family, geographic, or ethnic background (Caution: be careful with using ethnic humor so that you don't offend.)
- One of your annoying habits
- An embarrassing situation

You risk offending others if you make fun of the venue, the client, or others in the audience. So why not make a little fun of yourself? You can disclose anything you want as long as it supports your message, doesn't offend others, and doesn't undermine your credibility on the topic. You are both the easiest and safest subject for your humor!

FINDING THE COMMON GROUND ⚠️ ⚠️ ⚠️

Unlike a nightclub comedian, corporate presenters are typically speaking to an audience that has something in common. Whether or not you are part of the same organization, industry, or profession, you have common ground on which you can build humor. Figure out what those shared characteristics are so you can pick subjects about which your listeners are willing to laugh. Here are some generic subjects.

THE BOSS. Everybody has a boss. Some are even married to one. (See how this works?) You can make fun of the generic "boss" easily even if everyone has a different boss. If you are speaking to a group that has the same boss, it's a good idea to find out if that individual is okay with you having some fun with her. There are *former* managers all over the country who didn't check this out first.

POPULAR OR WELL-KNOWN PEOPLE. Look for people your participants *all* know. It could be the CEO, a supervisor, a top salesperson, or even the receptionist. Better yet, comment on the barista at the Starbucks in the building. You can even focus on celebrities and media stars.

Again, where applicable, test it out with those involved and make sure they can laugh about it. You wouldn't want to inadvertently make fun of the most beloved person in the organization or a celebrity who happens to be the company spokesperson.

HOT SPOTS. The meeting room, the hotel room (if they are all staying at the same hotel), the cafeteria, and the local watering hole are all potential subjects of humor. For example, there's one stylish hotel where the shower has only half a door. You could start your presentation in a hotel like that by saying, "I spent my entire morning at Lost and Found trying to find the rest of my shower door."

JARGON THEY USE. Every group has its own arcane vernacular, and that generally includes a multitude of acronyms. Do your research and work some humor into your presentation about this. For some unknown reason, the National Speakers Association always lists the initials of academic titles

and specific achievements when introducing their members. For instance, Kristin Arnold, MBA, CMC, CPF, CSP. Once an introducer welcomed Joe Speaker, PhD, CSP, CPAE, EIEIO. The audience loved it.

CURRENT EVENTS. National or local events that are front-page news, or current events within the company, make great subjects for humor. Caution: be sure you know the organization's stand on these events so that you don't represent the wrong view.

PARODY. Change the words of a recognizable song, poem, or quotation and insert specific material for the group. You can even put the words on slides and get the audience to sing along. And as an added bonus, the worse you sing, the funnier it can be.

LAUGHTER IN THE MOMENT

Steve Rizzo, CSP, CPAE Speaker Hall of Fame

I realized how powerful laughter can be when I taught eighth-grade English on Long Island, New York. Believe me, you *needed* a sense of humor. I knew that the attention span of the average student was about twenty minutes out of a forty-five-minute class, at best. Quite often I reverted to humor to get my students back into the lesson plan. There was one class in particular that I remember. We were going over the soliloquies of Shakespeare, and no one was paying attention. Without missing a beat, I went into Sylvester Stallone as Hamlet. "Ahh to be or ahh . . .not to be. Ahh that is ahh the question. Or is it the answer? Anyway whether it is nobler in the minds of ahh . . .oh ahh . . .I'd like to be a vowel. Yeah, the letter Yo."

I immediately got their attention and they returned to the lesson plan. What else could I have done to get their attention? Well, I could have slammed my book down on the desk and yelled: "You people better pay attention, because if you don't you are going to fail the test! Now, I want everyone's eyes focused on me right now!" I might have had their eyes looking at me, but would they have been paying attention? My ability to make them laugh helped me enjoy my job and helped them enjoy the process, which I believe helped them to absorb more information.

NATURAL HUMOR

UNIVERSAL ISSUES. Think of common, everyday trials and tribulations that most people in your audience can identify with. Almost everyone has been married or experienced a significant relationship. Almost everyone drives a car, goes to the doctor, has had a bad hair day, has too much e-mail to read, plays computer Solitaire—see how easy it is to think of universal issues?

KEEP YOUR HUMOR EYES OPEN ⚠

The easiest way to add humor to any presentation is to see it in the world around us. There is humor everywhere. We run into odd, offbeat, humorous situations daily. By simply paying attention, you open yourself up to an amazing world of humorous possibilities. However, most of us just don't remember these odd bits of humor that we saw less than two hours earlier. So what do you do? Carry a pen and paper with you and write it down so you can remember it when you need to. For example, Ron Culberson, a professional speaker and humorist in the healthcare industry, shares a sign he observed on the door of a doctor's office. It said: "Dr. Joseph Smith. Eye, ear, nose, and throat. Rear Entrance."

Jay Leno took being on the lookout for humor nationally. He had a recurring segment on the *Tonight Show* during which he shared funny headlines or signs that people had sent in. Basically, he was capitalizing on the humor that other people saw. A classic one is from a jewelry store that said, "Ears Pierced While You Wait." Like you have a choice?

For most of us, it simply requires paying more attention to the simple things that have potential for humor. Look for these things at home with your family, when you're out with your friends, or while you're at work. You could even ask friends, colleagues, and total strangers to recount funny or amusing events that happened to them—and then ask permission to use them.

You can also draw from the well of your past experiences. Make a list of all the potentially funny stories from your life (see chapter 10). When you started to drive. When you proposed to your spouse. When you changed your first diaper. Then, look at the point you are trying to make and match the stories to the point. You can share the funny thing that happened to you and invite others to laugh along with you.

OTHER SOURCES OF HUMOR

While your own personal stories are the best sources for keeping your material unique, you can also borrow humor from other sources. Newspapers, magazines, books, late-night TV shows, radio, movies, sports, billboards, advertisements, road signs, bumper stickers, cartoons, quotations, and humor anthologies are all great sources for humorous bits.

There are two dangers, however, whenever you borrow humor or adapt the story to make it fit your own presentation: (1) the audience may have heard it before (groan!), or what's worse, (2) if you try to pass it off as if it happened to you the audience could lose trust in you (double groan!).

When borrowing humor, *always* acknowledge the source. "I was listening to George Campbell, a professional speaker, who was talking about the value of failure. He said, 'Thomas Edison knew the value of failure. In his journal, it said that he failed a thousand times trying to develop the lightbulb. At least we *think* that's what it said. He wrote it in the dark.'"

NATURAL HUMOR

THE RISKS OF BORROWED HUMOR

The following story is true but the names were changed to protect the guilty. A professional speaker named Bob gave a presentation for a group of newer speakers that included a speaker named Jim. About six months later, Jim and Bob were speaking at the same conference. Unfortunately, Bob was unaware that Jim had told one of Bob's stories the day before. When Bob told the same story, the meeting planner came up to Bob and said that it is very unprofessional to steal other people's stories!

THE PURE HUMOR OF SPONTANEOUS INTERACTION

Some of the richest and funniest humor is created when you interview people during your program. By creating conversations on the spot that the rest of the audience listens in on (see chapter 6), you can earn huge laughs. Remember, it's about connecting first and being funny second. They know that these parts of the program cannot be totally rehearsed, and because they are witnessing the unfolding with you, the connection you form with them is even deeper.

HOW TO GET THE LAUGHS STARTED

Brad Montgomery, CSP

There are a three opportune times to start a dialogue with an audience member in order to make a connection with the larger audience.

The first is straightforward. You get a helper from his seat to join you to make a point. Or take an informal poll. "How many people have ever had that happen to them?" or even, "How many people think the cookies on that break were awesome?" While hands are up, single out somebody and ask a follow-up question. "What was the worst part about it for you?" or "When is the last time you had cookies that good?" Comedians use this transition frequently.

When they know they are planning to talk about jobs, comedians first ask the audience, "Who's got a job they love?" Somebody yells, "I do—I'm a courier." Now the comic has a real reason to talk to that guy. "Courier, no kidding, how did you get that job?"

The conversation goes from there. Eventually the comedian will roll into the prepared material about jobs.

Couldn't you do the same, no matter what you talk about? Perhaps you're a sales presentation speaker. Instead of launching into your section about IRAs, you could say, "How many people have an IRA?" Then turn to somebody and follow up: "What is your dream for retirement?" The connection is made with that person and the audience, it's lively and interactive, and many times it gets a laugh.

You can also follow up on whatever interaction you are already doing. Interview the volunteer for an exercise or a game. Or ask someone to help write on an easel chart or to "report back" on what her group did in the small-group exercise (see chapter 11 for more ideas).

A third way to transition into an interview is the boldest, but works great. Imagine you have three points to your message, and you've just finished up the second one. Point to an individual in the audience and interview them. No, I'm not kidding. Just do it. You can do it from the stage or as you come down into the audience, but just start asking questions.

"Hi, thanks for being here today. What do you do?"

"I'm in records."

"What is the most exciting or surprising part of your job?"

Now, again, this is where you cannot lose, because any answer they give you will be good. They will say something heartwarming like, "I work with people I love." Or maybe they'll say something funny like, "I get to steal all the Post-it notes I need." Either way, you get further connection—and the chance for easy humor.

And nearly always you can find a way to transition from this interview to your third point in your presentation. It might be something like, "Well, the fact that this person loves her workmates is going to make my next point easy for her. My next point is . . .blah, blah, blah." (Note: please insert your "next point" for the "blah, blah, blah." If you don't, your audience will think you've lost it.) It might sound scary, but the interview technique is easier than it seems, and the rewards are huge. Pick some transitions, go with some prepared questions, and you'll be surprised by how much closer your audience feels to you and how many laughs you get without writing a single punch line.

NATURAL HUMOR

WHAT ABOUT JOKES? ⚠️ ⚠️ ⚠️ ⚠️ ⚠️

Many years ago, jokes were the staple of professional speaking. More recently, though, the Internet has made jokes more available to the general public. So, there is always the risk that your audience has heard a particular joke. But you may still want to tell a joke because it fits the material. If so, to make your joke more successful avoid these common joke pitfalls:

- Do *not* announce that you are going to tell a joke.
- Never apologize for a bad joke before you even begin.

- Avoid jokes that have nothing to do with your presentation. That's not a joke; it's a distraction.

- Do not tell jokes that may insult someone or—worse—everyone.

- Avoid sexist, ethnic, political, racist, religious, ageist, weightist, heightist, and ugliest jokes or humor about a physical or mental disability. Unless you're a skilled humorist, you should stay away from potentially offensive humor.

- Do not tell a joke that drags out. The rule of thumb is the longer the joke, the funnier the punch line better be.

- Do not garble the punch line. Deliver a clear, exact punch line.

- Never laugh your way through the joke. It's okay to have enthusiasm for the joke, and it's okay to chuckle or laugh after the joke, but laughing before the audience even gets it is just bizarre.

- Never explain the punch line when your joke bombs. Chances are the audience won't even get it after the explanation.

- Don't panic or criticize the audience if they don't laugh at a particular joke. Some jokes fall flat. Simply move on or make fun of yourself for the lack of laughter.

WHAT TO DO WHEN HUMOR BOMBS

Every professional humorist and comedian has dealt with failed humor. They wouldn't be successful if they hadn't. But what they know that most of us don't is that a "saver line" can help the pain of the bombed humor. A saver line is something you use only when the humor bombs. For instance, if you tell a joke and nobody laughs, the audience feels awkward. You can say, "It's a good thing that wasn't supposed to be funny." The saver line gets the laugh. The audience has recovered and you can move on. You can find books that will give you examples of saver lines. Most pros have a dozen such lines in their back pocket.

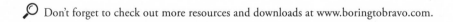 Don't forget to check out more resources and downloads at www.boringtobravo.com.

CHAPTER EIGHT RECAP

The only thing worse than bombing with humor is bombing without humor! These days, it's practically impossible to engage an audience without some form of humor. So, start with the right frame of mind and assume that humor is necessary for your success.

- Find the humor that works for you. Your humor must fit you.
- Trust that once you've found the fit, it will work.
- Use a type of humor that fits the topic, the situation, and the group.
- Use subjects about which everyone can relate by enhancing your observational skills.
- Find humor in your own life, the newspapers, a funny joke, or from a friend.
- Take advantage of humor to make your presentations come alive.
- So, should you use humor in your presentation? Only if you want to be effective.

ACTION PLAN

Based on the information in this chapter, I intend to

Continue _____

Start _____

Stop _____

NATURAL HUMOR

CHAPTER NINE

CHOOSE DESCRIPTIVE WORDS

DID YOU KNOW there are approximately 500,000 words in the *Oxford English Dictionary* but the typical presenter uses merely 2,000 of them? We use less than one percent of the available words in the English language, and that does not even include combinations, word derivatives, and technical and scientific terms yet to be cataloged. There are so many words to choose from, yet we rely on the few overused ones that seem to roll off our tongues and out of our mouths so easily.

Why not try (literally) a few bon mots that more eloquently tell the story or describe the situation? Reach beyond your comfort zone and deliberately choose descriptive words to bring your concepts to life and pique your audience's interest. Now, I am not suggesting that you peruse your handy thesaurus, looking for exotic words the average person typically doesn't hear too often, or even at all. But you can select a few choice words using some of the techniques in this chapter.

ANCHOR YOUR MAIN IDEA ⚠ ⚠

An anchor holds a ship in place. Tethered to a long rope, the flukes dig deep into the ocean floor, to keep the ship from drifting. You can create an "anchor" for your presentation in the form of a memorable theme, concept, or principle that holds your presentation together and remains long after your presentation is over. It can be one word, a phrase, a sound bite, or a statement that captures the essence of your speech or reinforces your call to action. It might be an acronym or acrostic that is easily remembered, with each letter representing a key idea within your presentation. It could also be a symbol or gesture that recurs during your presentation.

"Film directors know that if people walk out of your movie repeating a phrase they heard, that movie will make money," says Garry Marshall, Hollywood movie director (*Pretty Woman*). "It means audience members are taking the movie home with them. They're talking about it around the office watercooler and to their friends." When you speak, do audience members walk out repeating something specific you said?

Master negotiator Brad McRae anchors his key point—"You can't change someone's mind if you don't know where their mind is"—by using a group activity. Brad asks the participants to shake hands with a partner as if they had just been introduced while repeating the mantra. Brad explains: "The purpose of this exercise is to anchor the words through hearing, but also kinesthetically in the feel of the handshake. The principle is further reinforced because handshaking is symbolic of agreement."

You know you have really anchored your message when you start saying the phrase and the participants finish it with you. Your anchor "phrase that pays" will be remembered long after your presentation is over.

REPETITION, RESTATEMENT, AND THE RULE OF THREE ⚠ ⚠

Unfortunately, audiences do not always pay attention to you. Their minds wander. They think about the 462 e-mails in their inbox and their upcoming medical appointment. They could even be so preoccupied that they miss whole sections of your speech. Help them remember the salient points of your presentation with the 3Rs: Repetition, Restatement, and the Rule of Three:

- Repetition. People don't remember things well unless you strongly state your key points more than once. If you have an important word, phrase, or sentence, repeat it. Not just once, but at least three times. They are bound to hear it sometime during your presentation.

- Restatement. For variety, you can also restate your point with a different approach. "Let's look at that another way." You don't want to sound like a broken record (or is that a scratched disc these days?).

- Rule of Three. It is simply easier for your audience members to remember things in a group of three. Not two and not four. The magic number is three. They can remember three things, and the side benefit is that you can remember three things, too! For example, we say, "stop, look, and listen," "good, better, best," and even "snap, crackle, and pop." Think in terms of three to help your audience remember:

  - Three points
  - Three subpoints to each point
  - Three characteristics.

When using a group of three elements, arrange the words, phrases, or clauses in a sequence of increasing impact, with the strongest element (the climax) at the end. Or, to be a bit amusing, make the third point or subpoint a bit incongruous. For example, "To be a success, remember these three keys: be willing to take risks; learn from your mistakes; and i before e except after c."

USE STRONG WORDS

Not that you want to go back to grade school, but your grammar teacher (mine was Mrs. Clark, with a neat, compact bun on the crown of her head) emphasized the importance of a strong, active voice where the subject takes responsibility to act or do something. Passive voice, on the other hand, has the subject receiving the action. Here are two examples, both positive, but notice the punch in the first one: "The presenter engaged the audience" rather than "The audience was engaged by the presenter."

Similarly, when you feel strongly about something, be declarative. Use strong verbs to assert your ideas and opinions persuasively: "I know . . ." or "I am confident that . . ." Don't say "If this happens"; say "When this happens . . ."

Beware of fluffy words that don't say much of anything. What's a fluffy word? Common examples are "really," "very," "some," "a lot," "so," "definitely," and "surely"—all of which actually weaken the descriptive adjective that follows them. "That PowerPoint slide show was outdated" is a stronger statement than "That PowerPoint slide show was really/very/so outdated."

Vocalized hiccups are wimpy words that fill the air when you don't know what to say next or are clumsily making a transition from one point to another. Here are two ideas to help you eliminate such filler words as "well," "uh," "umm," "ah," "you know," "like," and "but," from your presentations:

1. Replace them with silence. After all, they are just vocalized hiccups.

2. Take a tip from Toastmasters: When practicing, have a friend ring a bell or make some other noise every time you use a filler word. It takes only a speech or two to eliminate these distracting audible pauses.

Stay away from wimpy words that make you look unsure and uncertain. They insert a niggling question in each participant's mind as to why they should bother listening to you. You've heard these words and phrases often: "perhaps," "maybe," "hopefully," "seems like," "you know," "sort of," "kind of"—you get the idea.

CHOOSE VIVID WORDS

Vivid words paint a mental picture in each audience member's mind. Such words convert the mundane into the memorable. They engage the audience in the moment and live long after the conclusion of your presentation.

MENTAL IMAGERY. Your word choice is critical because the brain thinks in pictures, not words. Some presenters may show the actual picture, but you can engage your audience by crafting word pictures. Choose words that stir your audience's imagination and create a level of detail so each person can see it in their mind's eye. When you describe something vividly, people will conjure up images that are important to them—which may not be what you saw at all! (But that's okay, because it is not about you; your speech is about them.)

EXPERIMENT: USE DESCRIPTIVE WORDS

Consider these word groups made up of nouns, adjectives, and verbs. Which words paint a more vivid picture for you? What image does each word bring to mind?

Man	hobo, prince, surfer
Dog	Labrador retriever, puppy, Lassie
Phone	rotary dial phone, iPhone, car phone
Shiny	glittery, polished, burnished
Speak	yell, whisper, hiss
Run	jog, lope, gallop

VISUAL BLEND. When conjuring up a visual that is new to others, take two or three familiar visuals and combine them. For example, when describing a character the audience doesn't know, you could say, "She's a cross between Oprah Winfrey and Tiger Woods."

UNEXPECTED. You can also choose a novel word or two that surprises people because it is so unexpected. It could be a word choice that deviates from a common phrase or boring cliché. For example, wouldn't you be surprised if you heard someone describe the weather by saying "it was raining cats and kibbles"? Bill Cates, author of *Get More Referrals Now!*, when referring to his age says, "People of my vintage . . ." It is a slight turn of the phrase that captures our attention.

Beware of using an interesting, novel word or phrase too often, however. The first time you say "cow patty" instead of the slang word for manure, it will sound fresh. The second time is still mildly interesting, but by the sixth or seventh time, it will be stinky!

Similarly, you want to choose words that everyone in your audience can understand. They shouldn't need a dictionary to keep up with you. If you choose to use an otherwise erudite term that no one will comprehend out of the context of your speech, use it sparingly!

EXAGGERATION. If you choose to exaggerate a situation that everyone can relate to as a way of making your point, be sure to grossly magnify the features so it is an *obvious* untruth. There should never be a question in the audience's mind as to whether there is a grain of truth in your exaggerated statement.

DESCRIPTIVE WORDS

EXPERIMENT: USE VIVID WORDS!

Describe to yourself the room or space you are in right now. How did you describe it? Try it again, describing it differently. How does it look? Now describe how it sounds. How does it feel? Here's the zinger—how does it taste?

Think about your word choices. Did you choose

♦ vivid over bland?

♦ specific over general?

♦ novel over commonplace?

ARRANGE WORDS RHYTHMICALLY TO RESONATE WITH YOUR AUDIENCE ⚠

When choosing vivid words, arrange them to resonate with a pleasing rhythm and sound to the ear. Rhythm is the arrangement of words, vocalization, and silence to create an emotional balance that spurs the audience to continue to listen to you.

CADENCE VARIATION. Think of the cadence of your sentences. If all of your sentences are short, your speech will sound like an automatic machine gun. If all of them are long, no one will be able to follow you. Strike a balance. Contrast the two frequently to keep your audience's attention.

ALLITERATION. The repetition of usually initial consonant sounds in two or more neighboring words within successive sentences or paragraphs can make a strong impression on your listeners. Promising that a small group activity will be "wacky and wild" or "frantic but fun," for example, will perk up their ears. Or asking your audience to watch out for the "three things that you must do today" will certainly pique their curiosity.

PARALLEL CONSTRUCTION. Create balance within a phrase or sentence or among several sentences by using parallel construction. It provides a consistent structure for your ideas that helps you fit them into the file folders of each listener's mind. For example, if the title of your speech is "Seven Strategies to Help You Engage Your Audience," be sure to introduce each strategy with its corresponding number. And your description of each strategy should follow a consistent, identical pattern and typically start with a noun or a verb. Just look at the many bulleted lists in this book for examples of parallel construction. So dust off your grammar books, stay parallel, and keep the audience on track with you.

EXPERIMENT: CADENCE EXERCISE

Take a page from your speech and count the number of words in each sentence. Write the numbers down and average them. Note the highest and lowest number of words you use. Read your longest sentence aloud, and then read your shortest sentence aloud. Which one is more engaging and memorable? If you average twenty or more words per sentence, you are putting in too many words. The result? Your message is getting lost.

DESCRIPTIVE WORDS

THE POWER OF THE PAUSE ⚠️ ⚠️

Consider this: While you deliver valuable information, your audience needs to absorb what you are saying. A well-placed pause allows your audience to reflect on your words for a brief moment in time. A pause enables them to create connections between what they are hearing and what they already know.

THE POWER OF THE PAUSE

Lou Heckler, CSP, CPAE Speaker Hall of Fame

Most speakers get excited or nervous when speaking before a group and miss the chance to use a pause to create all sorts of additional enjoyment for an audience. Let's make it easy and say the pause is as simple as A-B-C.

A is "Allow ideas to sink in." Really effective speakers think of their presentations as a dialogue rather than a monologue—even though the audience may not actually be speaking. When we take a few extra beats after a particularly powerful story or when offering a plausible solution to a problem we're discussing, we encourage audience members to silently say, "Yes . . . that makes sense . . . I can think of a place or two in my life where I can use this."

B is "Build anticipation." Think game shows on TV. On most of them, a question is posed and a contestant has to come up with the right answer. As the stakes get higher, the host usually waits a few beats more before confirming the answer or not. We at home get more interested and excited as the wait goes on. Your audiences will do the same. I have a story I share about teaching my son how to drive. We have come to a place where both he and I might get crushed by a truck if I don't give him really good, quick instructions from my passenger seat. To build anticipation, I first explain to the audience that I used some long, drawn-out speech to advise him to pull out of the way. They know darn well I probably yelled something fast and loud, and when I finally confess (and show them what I did), their anticipation has gathered so much steam that as I yell, "Get Over! Get Over!" they burst out laughing and applaud like crazy.

C is "Cause the blanks to be filled in." Audiences like to "play" along with you; that is, they *like* to guess what comes next and *love* to be right. I have a story I love to tell about an encounter with a couple of bikers at a fast-food restaurant. The one fellow is wearing some kind of mohair vest and no shirt, but when I start to describe him, I fumble a bit and say, "He was wearing a . . . uh . . ." and I make the motions around my upper body to indicate a vest. Invariably, someone in the audience, wishing to fill in the blank, yells out, "Vest!" Then I get a laugh by saying, "No . . . I think it might have been an animal at one time!"

Go through your material and see where you can slow down here and there and use the A-B-C approach to insert some effective pauses. Your audience will love it—and so will you.

LISTS, HEADLINES, AND HIGHLIGHTS ⚠

Take a tip from David Letterman. Audiences *love* lists. Why? Because they provide a structure not only for your presentation but also for your participants to follow. Yes, a list will help you stay on track, but more important, it helps the audience know where you are going.

To make your list most effective, tell your audience the number of points, and then step through each one, enumerating each point as you go:

- Headlines. Each point should be in "headline" form—a phrase of no more than five words that encapsulates your idea. Encourage your audience to write each point down in order to solidify the learning.

- Highlights. Provide focus and emphasis by calling direct attention to the important thing you want them to remember. Use a phrase such as, "A particularly important factor . . ."

Your list, with its great headlines and highlights, is also easy for your audience to send to each other using Twitter. Your well-honed one-liners fit within the 140-character-tweeting boundary and would be snappy reading for those unable to attend your presentation.

USE WORDS THAT SELL ⚠ ⚠

According to Abraham Maslow and a passel of direct marketers, certain words strike an emotional chord and move people to action. Figure out what your audience cares about and which words you can use to engage them at their emotional and psychological levels.

Integrate the following words into your speech and you will have your listeners hooked:

- Self-Actualization/Fulfillment
  - Results/Gain—This is the bottom line. You tell people, or help them discover, the benefits they will receive or gain as a result of listening to you.
  - Ego—You receive affirming recognition from others.

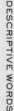

DESCRIPTIVE WORDS

- New/Improved—Everyone loves getting something new or knowing something new. Of course, if it is *not* new, but simply repackaged, go for the word "improved" or "enhanced."

- Social/Belonging
  - Love/Like—Though love makes the world go round, it doesn't typically work well in work situations. Use sparingly, but you can easily substitute the word "like."
  - Easy—Who wouldn't want something to make their life easier?
  - Yes—We adore the word "yes" because it gives permission; it agrees with us and says we are right.

- Safety/Security
  - Save—Most business cases revolve around saving time or money. Show how you can save time or money or both, and you will definitely have your group's attention.
  - Guarantee—Most people are not risk takers, so take away the fear of the unknown by guaranteeing your promise.
  - Proven—Demonstrate that something has already been tested and proven successful.
  - Money—Poll any audience about what they wish they could have more of and money (and what it can buy) would be number one. Money can't buy you happiness, but it sure can buy a lot of trinkets.

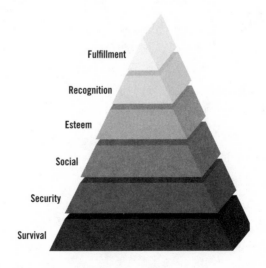

- Free—You've immediately got my attention! Many folks, however, believe that nothing is really "free"; there is always a catch. Let them know what it is.
- Physiological Needs/Survival
  - You—The most powerful word that sells is "you." Personalize your presentation and use this word often.

KEEP IT SIMPLE

Some people believe they must utilize pedantic multisyllabic words to sound erudite and thus to effectuate a stellar impression. (A little irony there; did you get it?) If you hear yourself using more than a few obscure words, define them immediately so the audience doesn't get hung up, thinking, "What does she mean?"

LESS IS MORE

Pull out your speech and sharpen your pencil. If you don't have a presentation to edit, then record yourself actually giving a speech. Make a transcript of the speech and scratch out all the words you could have left out. Needless to say, this is quite a humbling experience—regardless of your level of expertise!

Continue editing your presentation:

1. Replace pretentious words with simple words any Jack or Jill can understand.

2. Make your point using as few words as possible. Try combining several words, deleting a few, or dreaming up a new turn of phrase.

3. Delete redundancies and fluffy words that add nothing to your presentation.

4. Delete Dilbert-style corporate buzzwords that lack substance. These include hackneyed phrases such as "think outside the box," "institute a paradigm shift," "take the 30,000-foot view," or "bite the bullet." Should you want to make fun of these clichés, turn to chapter 8 on using humor in your presentations.

DESCRIPTIVE WORDS

5. Limit the organizational jargon. Steeped in the content of their own technical presentations, many speakers assume that their listeners know the jargon, abbreviations, and arcane terminology well. They don't. So define the term up front and use it sparingly. Try not to have more than one corporate acronym in a sentence.

6. Challenge yourself to find another way to explain something so others who are not as well versed in the topic can get it.

7. Examine your word groupings (remember the Rule of Three) to sequence the elements and place the strongest at the end.

8. Examine your entire speech for parallel construction.

 Don't forget to check out more resources and downloads at www.boringtobravo.com.

CHAPTER NINE RECAP

 Test your understanding of all the different types of stories you can tell by filling in the blank.

1. Anchor your _____ idea.

2. Remember the 3Rs: Repetition, _____ , and the Rule of Three.

3. Use active voice over _____ voice.

4. Omit fluffy words, vocalized _____ , and wimpy words.

5. Arrange sentences to create a pleasant cadence and _____ .

6. Don't forget the power of the _____ .

7. Make use of a _____ with pithy headlines and highlights.

8. KISS. Keep It _____ , Silly!

ACTION PLAN

Based on the information in this chapter, I intend to

Continue _____

Start _____

Stop _____

DESCRIPTIVE WORDS

TELL INTERESTING STORIES

ONCE UPON A TIME . . .

What happened to you physically as you read those words? If you are like most people, you exhaled; you released the tension in your shoulders as you prepared to listen to a story.

Next time you are at a presentation, watch how a simple story can bring an audience to life. You can actually see a visible change in the audience when you tell a story that humanizes and personalizes your topic. Most participants will lean forward, smile, and either nod their heads to agree or shake their heads to disagree. Your audience may not remember exactly what you said during your presentation, but they *will* remember your stories.

When listeners hear a well-told story, they take a journey with you, correlating their own experiences with yours. Your story becomes their story or it reminds them of a very similar story from their own lives. We call this a "Me Too Moment." Your stories help you build a connection to your audience. Here is the weird part, however: After one of my presentations, a participant will share his Me Too Moment, which is a vastly different story from my own and with a different meaning altogether! I used to think these participants just didn't get my point, but I eventually realized that they got the point *they* needed to get. That is what is so great about stories: each of your participants can derive his or her own unique takeaway from the same story.

Stories create the quintessential bonding experience between a speaker and the audience. When you can, share a personal story, but be sure to talk about the attributes of the story that will interest *the audience*. (This is the hard part because the aspects of your story that *you* love might not be relevant to your audience.) Choose descriptive words (see chapter 9) using the names of actual persons, places, or events. Give your story an ample sprinkling of color and life.

Because audience members feel powerfully connected through stories, you should aim to have at least one compelling story at either the beginning or the end of your speech. You can also use a relevant story to support each of your points. Now, I know what you're thinking. "I don't have time to tell a story!" Yes, you do, and really, you must. Even short speeches can benefit from a "short story" because, as you'll come to realize from reading this chapter, stories come in all shapes and sizes. A story can range from something as simple as a quotation or a testimonial, an example or an analogy, a simple fact or a relevant statistic, to a full-blown personal anecdote that has a beginning, a middle, and an ending.

EXPERIMENT:
BE ON THE LOOKOUT FOR STORIES

In the next few business presentations, note who uses stories and when they use them. At the same time, watch the audience. How does the story transform the audience? Do people become more receptive? Curious? Engaged? Connected?

DEFINITIONS, QUOTATIONS, AND TESTIMONIALS ⚠

DEFINITIONS

If a concept or term may not be familiar to your listeners, define it for them. You can start with a boring definition from the dictionary and then describe the term using everyday words. Or be imaginative and think up your own definition. Or think of the first time you encountered the concept and describe what you thought it meant; then follow up with the real definition and discuss the similarities and differences.

QUOTATIONS

Quote an expert's eloquent statement about your subject. This technique lends credibility from from the source as well as from the actual phrase in support of your point. Try to pick a quotation that is relevant to your topic, witty, memorable, and attributed to a famous person or a local personality. 🔍

You can likewise mention the names of famous or important people you actually know firsthand or have an indirect connection with as a means of complementing your point and lending credibility to your coverage of the subject. Use this technique sparingly, though, because your audience could interpret your name-dropping as a supercilious ego boost.

- Use aphorisms/proverbs. Phrases that everybody knows, like "haste makes waste," are useful communication shortcuts that don't require a source.

- Adapt. You can repurpose a well-known quote or proverb to change the meaning to support your point. For example, in concluding his Franklin Time Management Workshop, Hyrum Smith admonishes the group: "Practice makes *perfect*? No, practice makes *permanent*, so practice right!" (He further teases the audience with a "fill in the blank" technique that leaves the word "perfect" to be replaced with their own choices.)

- Cite the source. If you don't know for sure who said it, say something along the lines of: "I believe it was _____ who said . . ." or "Someone once said . . ."

INTERESTING STORIES

- Include cultural icons. You can use memorable lines that reflect the current culture and that your audience will be familiar with. Sources for such lines include TV sitcoms, advertisements, commercials, and movies. For instance, "You're in good hands"; "Don't leave home without it"; or even the famous Clint Eastwood challenge, "Make my day."

- Create your own. You can always make up a quote that pulls the audience into your story. You could say, "My wild and crazy Uncle Ned always said . . ." and dispense his words of wisdom. Of course, it is much better if your Uncle Ned actually uttered the statement, or said something similar.

TESTIMONIALS

When a respected expert or authority has made a statement in support of your position or will serve as a reference, you have more than a quote; you have *corroborating evidence*—that is, proof, in someone else's words, that supports your view.

EXAMPLES, ILLUSTRATIONS, AND CASE STUDIES ⚠

EXAMPLES

Examples are short statements to clarify or elaborate on your point that are usually expressed in one or two sentences. They are often prefaced with "for example" or "for instance."

Try to refer to specific people in the room or the audience as a whole to demonstrate or make your point. An example of this would be "You can engage your audience using myriad techniques. For example, you can interview an audience member or take a poll."

ILLUSTRATIONS

When you're looking to extend an example, use an illustration to provide more detail in order to clarify your point. The best illustrations use specific names, dates, and locations, as appropriate. Generally, an illustration describes a process or chronology of events and provides a level of concreteness that is easily remembered. "Sally really engages her audiences. How? Let me give you an illustration. At the presentation last week, she interviewed three audience members, including the CEO . . ."

CASE STUDIES

Detailed stories that are based on an intensive analysis of a person or a community within a given environment are called case studies. You can use these to provide support for the point you are trying to make. You can cite your own hard-learned scenarios or purchase them from management review journals. Harvard Business School, for example, is famous for publishing case studies wherein a problem situation is outlined and various experts weigh in on what should be done.

- Tee up the case study as a problem to be solved and let the participants share their opinions about what should be done.

- Describe the starting assumptions and let the participants identify what the problems are.

- Provide two or three suitable solutions and let the participants discuss the advantages and disadvantages of each alternative.

- If you are going to create your own case studies, remove all explicit or indirect references to the parties involved that could lead to the identification of the organization or individual.

COMPARISONS, ANALOGIES, AND ALLUSIONS ⚠ ⚠

We all have a figurative file drawer that contains all of the information we know. And it is easier to take in new information when we can relate it to something that resides in that file drawer. Comparisons, analogies, and allusions help listeners pull out the right file and add additional information to their knowledge base.

INTERESTING STORIES

COMPARISONS

Put briefly, comparisons show similarities whereas contrasts show differences. Use comparisons when you want to reveal similar characteristics, features, and qualities; use contrasts when you want to present how one set of conditions differs from another.

Some common comparisons and contrasts are

- Is/is not—"This is what it is; this is what it is not."
- Retrospective/prospective—"That was then; this is now."
- Point/counterpoint—"Issues for; issues against."
- Review/preview—"Here's where we have been, and here's where we are going."

ANALOGIES

An analogy is a comparison of two things to highlight some strong point or points they have in common. Analogies are often used in technical presentations as a way to connect the unknown (what you are presenting) to something the audience already knows. There are basically two ways we express an analogy:

1. A simile compares two things that are not the same and are not normally considered together. The key words you'll use when using a simile are "like" or "as." For example, our brains are like a computer. As you read this book, your brain is storing information in your "buffer" just as your computer stores data. What happens when your computer crashes before you hit the Save button? You lose all that data.

2. A metaphor is a more direct version of a simile that talks about one thing as if it is the other. Take out the "like" or "as" and your simile becomes a metaphor. To continue the previous example, in order to retain the information in this book, you need to hit the Save button in your brain frequently or risk having an empty hard drive.

ALLUSIONS

When you allude to something, you are making brief, indirect references to a person, place, or event that everybody can identify. An allusion evokes a connection among three parties—you, the audience, and the image you are referencing—without saying who, what, or where it is.

Let's look at a few categories you can allude to in order to get your audience exploring rather than snoring:

- Politicians. Politicians are famous for serving up some phrases that stick. By mentioning the well-known phrase, there is a connection to that time and place in history. For example, "Ask not what your country can do for you, but what you can do for your country" evokes the memory of John F. Kennedy.

- Current events. You can allude to a current event at a local, regional, or national level. You can also tap into what is happening among the participants' organizations if that information is widely known.

- Celebrities. Some celebrities have enduring personalities. They may not be endearing, but they are well-known and thus worthy targets of allusion, even after they are long gone. When I am introduced, my "princess wave" to wordlessly say "hello" to the audience is an allusion to Princess Diana.

- Flashback. Refer, or call back, to something that was said earlier in the presentation, a question that was asked, or anything that might have occurred from the moment the audience entered the room.

FINDING THE RIGHT ANALOGY

Betsey Allen, MBA, CSP, CQM

A well-phrased analogy can exponentially enhance how your message gets remembered every time. Follow these simple rules and this example to create your own next memorable analogy:

1. Clarify the purpose and people. First, clarify whom the message is for and the outcome you are after. During the late 1990s, when the welfare laws changed, I oversaw the Welfare to Work Training in Lee County, Florida, and helped the boat builders in Fort Myers tap federal funding to put new wage earners to work as fiberglass handlers. My audience was primarily minority females who had probably never been in a boat much less knew anything about building one! Yet, within twenty-five hours, we needed them to know every step of building a boat, and we needed a visual memory hook that would stay top of mind as they became independent workers.

2. Define the elements, pieces, or parts. Fiberglass handling is messy work. It is done outdoors in the heat of summer, with hazardous chemicals and challenging conditions. The process uses wet (resin) and dry (reinforcement) ingredients that are temperamental. When used out of sequence or measured inaccurately, the combinations can start fires. In fact, if you do everything right, yet you don't have the fiberglass rubbed out within thirty minutes, you have to start over.

3. Brainstorm similes and metaphors. Analogies are everywhere. After brainstorming metaphors that were visual and could be connected to the audience and purpose, we landed on "building a boat is like baking a cake."

4. Narrow the potentials that link back to your purpose. You bake a cake from the inside out, just as you build a boat. You have wet and dry ingredients, which must be accurately measured and baked delicately to create a cake. The same holds true for a boat. Finally, the last step of the process is to rub out the fiberglass before it hardens just as you rub on the frosting while it's soft.

Selecting your analogy is more of an art than a science, but it takes a bit of thought to pick just the right one that resonates with your audience!

FACTS AND STATISTICS ⚠

One of my favorite TV characters is Cliff Claven on *Cheers*, the quirky postman who knows scads of meaningless trivia. He would say, "It's a little known fact . . ." and conclude with a pithy factoid. You, too, can engage the audience with an unusual, striking, and surprising fact or statistic to support and validate your topic. The key is to make it interesting to the audience. Your facts and statistics should tell a story, not be a stand-alone comment.

FACTS

To use an interesting factoid, you are going to have to do a bit of research.

- Topic. Serve up some interesting facts about your topic as a "Did you know . . . ?" or "Ever wonder why . . . ?"

- Audience. During your prework, you might have stumbled upon an interesting bit of trivia about a particular person in the group or the entire group.

- Location. Present some interesting facts about the venue or city that relate to your message.

- Benefits. Is there an interesting fact about the people who will benefit from your call to action that would be of interest to your listeners?

- Process. Is there something unique about how your topic is going to be accomplished?

- Benchmarks. Has someone else conducted the same or a similar kind of analysis on your topic that would be noteworthy to share?

- Current event. What is going on in the community, city, state, nation, or world that is interesting to your listeners? Check the morning newspaper, a professional journal, or a local news program, and link something that has recently made the news with your topic or within the industry.

- History. What happened in history on the specific date on which you are going to give your speech? Connect it to your theme or point of your presentation. 🔍

STATISTICS

Although you are intimately familiar with all of the numbers, take a look at your data from your audience's point of view. There must always be a compelling reason why the numbers you are presenting are important. It is your job to tell the story behind the numbers.

Create a way to make the statistic come to life and have meaning for the audience, emphasizing the truly important part of the fact, statistic, or trend.

PUT THE NUMBER IN A DAY-TO-DAY CONTEXT. Compare your statistic with some other well-known fact that can be easily understood by the audience. For example, "According to a study released by the U.S. Department of Education in 2009, 30 million American adults are functionally illiterate. That means one in seven of us is unable to read well enough to do our jobs, lead fulfilling lives, or even read a presentation handout."

ILLUSTRATE THE STATISTIC. In order for your audience to understand and visualize the enormity of the statistic, use visual images. Describe something as "the equivalent of two football fields end to end" so people can literally see the numbers and the length in their mind's eye.

I used to tell a story about the premature birth of my son, Travis. Most audiences couldn't comprehend just how tiny Travis was when I told them he weighed in at just 520 grams. So, I began to compare his birth length and weight to the size and weight of a sixteen-ounce can of soda. I could delicately place him in my hand, with the tip of his head at the tip of my fingers and his little legs dangling from the base of my palm. It made an even bigger impact when I held up a can of soda.

BE PRECISE. Round off the data if you want the audience to comprehend the number quickly; be more precise if you want to add to the believability of the statistic. Your audience may well forget the actual number you give, but they will easily remember the picture.

BE SPECIFIC. Beware of using the phrase "Many authorities declare . . ." Your audience will wonder who the authorities are. Be specific and name the source (or sources). Understand where and how the data were generated— just in case you get a question from the audience.

PERSONAL AND SIGNATURE STORIES ⚠ ⚠

PERSONAL STORY

Telling personal stories and anecdotes helps you create a connection with your audience and makes your point come to life. When you share a brief story based on your personal experiences, you create Me Too Moments where you share a common experience that your audience may have gone through or could have to live through. A personal story is uniquely your own. No one else has said it before, nor will your audience ever hear it from another speaker. It is the most sincere form of storytelling because you don't have to remember the lines; you just have to relive the story.

A note of caution is in order here: make sure you have worked through the issues, experienced the emotions (pain, anger, embarrassment, etc.), and can share with your audiences from a place of strength and peace. The platform should *not* be your therapy session, and your audiences *know* when you are still carrying around baggage. It's very uncomfortable and awkward for them, so don't do it. Give yourself some time to heal before you share the experience on center stage.

SIGNATURE STORY

When you become well-known because of one of your personal stories, you have developed a signature story. Audiences may even ask you to tell that one specific story because you tell it so well. Remember: *Never* ever copy another speaker's signature story or interaction. It's their story, so don't even try to adopt it as your own or adapt it for your own use.

INTERESTING STORIES

HOW TO DISCOVER THE UNIQUENESS IN YOUR PERSONAL HISTORY

Elizabeth Jeffries, CSP, CPAE Speaker Hall of Fame

Steve was a competent yet quiet executive. A lived-in-his-head kind of person, he wasn't exactly a dynamic communicator. Steve was charged by the CEO to rally the sales team at their national conference to do better and do more. He had lots of material and facts, but nothing to really grab the audience and get them to take action.

When I processed him through his personal history, he told me a story about growing up on a farm and what that meant to him. As he shared his story with me, his eyes sparkled, a smile lit up his face, and his whole body became engaged in the retelling of his memories. We had found something special indeed!

We polished the story, honed the message, and practiced the speech he wanted to share with the sales team. The initial sign of success came when I witnessed a line of salespeople forming after the program to talk to Steve. (A definite first for him.) I overheard one person tell Steve how his story reminded her of a similar experience, and she went on to tell him her story. The later sign of success came in the increased energy of the entire team and, consequently, more sales for this company! And so the story goes.

Everyone has a personal history and stories to tell about their life experiences and events. You do, and your audience does too. When you tap into those memories and share appropriate personal stories and illustrations with your audience, you'll connect with them on a new level. Your story sparks their story and they go with you on the journey of learning. Your authenticity, and even vulnerability, will move people from their heads to their hearts to take action on your ideas.

You may be objecting, "But I don't have any stories . . ." Oh yes you do! You have lots of them! The facts and experiences of your personal history may be poignant, painful, or playful. Here is how to discover your unique stories that will light up your audiences:

1. Identify six to ten of the most significant or memorable events in your life and look for the common denominator among them.

2. Benchmark your career history by listing all of your jobs and the roles you played or major activities you were involved in. What pattern do you see?

3. Use prompts to access your memories.

Plots—Can you remember a time when your first impression of someone turned out to be completely wrong?

Places—Take us to school with you during one of your most significant years or to a special childhood hiding place.

People—Introduce us to a teacher who had a profound impact on you; a person who taught you a lesson.

4. What is the point of learning in the story? There are probably several lessons you learned as result of your experience.

5. Draw upon your reservoir of stories and pick the most appropriate story for the specific audience you are speaking to. Each story should reinforce the key points made during your presentations.

BORROWED STORIES

Perhaps you don't have an original personal story or anecdote to share. That's okay; you may borrow other people's stories as long as you

1. Cite the source and ask their permission, if at all possible.
2. Share your personal story about how you encountered the individual or the anecdote.
3. Relive the moment when that individual's wisdom impacted you.
4. Relate the idea back to the audience so attendees can apply it to their personal circumstances.

When you borrow a story, rather than adopting it as your own, you are actually adapting it to be relevant to you and your audience. Now that is okay! You can find anecdotes just about everywhere.

PARTICIPANTS. Let's say, based on your prework interviews, that you uncover a story you're confident will make one of your points come to life. You can weave the story and the contributor's name (with permission, of course) into your presentation. The woman looks like a hero when you recognize her by asking her to stand up or by applauding her.

OBSERVATIONS. Based on your observations of the audience either during your prework or right before your presentation, you can tell a story about something that you personally witnessed.

PRINTED MATERIAL. Look through that folder of magazine and newspaper articles or that stack of books that are lying around. *USA Today*, the *Wall Street Journal*, and *Inc.* magazine are some of my favorites. Read stuff you don't normally read; you'll be amazed at the new connections you can make for your audiences. Clip those stories that are memorable to you, right along with the source information.

GOOGLE. The Internet offers a wealth of information in which to find just the right story and to check out facts and sources. Remember these caveats, however, in quoting material garnered in cyberspace:

- Legality. Look at the website's disclosure policy (usually located on the homepage) to ascertain the usage rights. When in doubt, ask for permission to use a specific chunk of material. Most folks will grant permission as long as you credit the source.

- Accuracy. It is tempting to share a story you heard long ago. Before you tell it, check it out and make sure your facts, figures, definitions, and sources are accurate. Finding and consulting the authorities on your subject may take a little time, but you don't want to lose credibility with your audience.

- Freshness. Just as you don't want to use the same overused clip art in your slide show presentation, you don't want to use a stale or overused story. How do you know? Test it out on a couple of participants before your presentation to see if they've heard it before.

INVITE THEM INTO YOUR STORY ⚠ ⚠ ⚠

As you rehearse telling your story, look for places where you can pause and invite the audience into your story.

WALK INTO THE AUDIENCE. While telling your story, purposefully walk into the audience and make eye contact with individuals. Look for agreement by using a participant's name. "Joe, would you agree with me that . . . ?" Whenever it's possible and plausible to do so, connect your story to the people in the audience.

PICTURE THIS. Ask the audience to picture a specific situation in their mind's eye. Try to put an audience member in the story, using vivid words.

- "Let's follow Roger as he does this, then that."
- "Come with me as my invisible partner . . ."
- "Picture this . . ." or "Imagine you are . . ."

HOW TO CONDUCT A VISUALIZATION EXERCISE

1. Ask the audience to close their eyes, relax, and begin breathing deeply.

2. Ask them to picture a place (a favorite place where they feel safe, relaxed, and comfortable), and give them a few moments to create that picture in their mind.

3. Ask them specific questions to crystallize the picture and their emotions.

4. After you have accomplished your objective, ask them to open their eyes.

5. Debrief by asking them to reflect on the experience or share with the person next to them how they felt.

INTERESTING STORIES

IN MEDIAS RES. Rather than starting your story at the beginning, drop your audience right into the middle of the action. It encourages them to catch up to you.

SHARE A BIT. Tell one bit, piece, or chunk of the story at a time. After each bit, ask the audience to reflect (or discuss) what might have been the next step. Then continue the story and reveal the next bit.

LEAVE 'EM HANGING. Tell part of the story and, at a particularly interesting moment, shift to another thread. Just remember to return to the end of the story.

FILL IN THE BLANK. Ask participants to fill in the blanks on your handout or in your speech with key words or phrases from a familiar story such as a fairy tale, a children's game, or lyrics to a holiday song. If you are speaking to a particular age group, use the lyrics to classic songs of their youth. The Beatles are always a classic, regardless of a person's age.

AUTORESPONDERS ⚠ ⚠

You can ask the audience to actually get involved in telling the story through a technique I call an "autoresponder." As part of your story, you expect or train the audience to respond with a specific answer. Here are some examples of different types of autoresponders.

SING-ALONGS. Think of a campfire sing-along (often a round). Have the audience follow and sing along with you.

REPEAT AFTER ME. Ask the group to make a pledge to you and their fellow participants as they commit to a new behavior. "I do solemnly swear . . ."

FILL IN THE BLANK. Let the audience finish your sentence with an extremely well-known phrase or answer. Roxanne Emmerich, culture transformation specialist, tells a story about when she first moved to Michigan and went shopping at the Mall of _____ (America). The shopkeepers would come up to her and say, "May I help you," and her answer would always be "No, thank you. Just _____ (looking)." The participants were able to fill in each pause as she would lean forward with the expectation that they would chime in with the obvious answer.

EXPRESSIONS. Create a specific "tag," such as an expression or physical movement. Give the audience a solid visible/audible queue for when they should respond by doing something you have trained them to do. For example, when Tim Gard, a laugh-out-loud humorist, puts two thumbs up, the participants are trained to say, "Woo hoo," and when he puts his hand to his forehead, they know to say "Bummer."

HEADLINES. Reduce your major points to "headlines" that your audience can easily recall or revisit when prompted. When Shep Hyken, an award-winning speaker on customer service, shares several examples of a "moment of misery" as opposed to a "moment of magic," after a few stories, the audience is calling out whether it is a moment of magic or a moment of misery. You know you have a phrase that pays when they can recall your headline long after your presentation!

HOW TO CREATE AN AUTORESPONDER

1. Ask. You have to ask for the group's permission. Jeff Tobe, a guru of innovation and change, asks his audiences to respond with an energetic "ABSOLUTELY" whenever they are in agreement with a question he asks the audience.

2. Model. Before you can expect the audience to follow you, model the behavior you want. Jeff shows them what an energetic "ABSOLUTELY" response sounds like. This is done in two places: during the request and in step number 3.

3. Affirmation. You can be patient and see if they pick up the mantra naturally, or you can ask for them to repeat it. Jeff simply asks, "Can you do that?" while leaning forward with the expectation that the audience will respond with the correct answer.

4. Reinforce. When you get a strong response, acknowledge it. When it is rather wimpy (which is usually the first or second time until the participants get it), Jeff will gently tease the audience into participating. It then becomes natural for the participants to listen for and respond to a question with an energetic "ABSOLUTELY!"

INTERESTING STORIES

 Don't forget to check out more resources and downloads at www.boringtobravo.com.

CHAPTER TEN RECAP

Match the different kinds of stories with the correct definition:

1. A comparison of two things that are alike in some ways and different in others.

2. A statement that can be verified, either by referring to a third source or by direct observation.

3. A word, phrase, sentence, or gesture that prompts the audience to respond with a specific answer.

4. An example that extends the explanation.

5. An anecdote or narrative taken from another source.

6. An anecdote or narrative based on your personal experiences.

7. A statement by someone who is usually an authority or expert in the subject.

A. Quotation

B. Illustration

C. Analogy

D. Fact

E. Personal Story

F. Borrowed Story

G. Autoresponder

ACTION PLAN

Based on the information in this chapter, I intend to

Continue _____

Start _____

Stop _____

Answers: 1-C; 2-D; 3-G; 4-B; 5-F; 6-E; 7-A

INVOLVE THE AUDIENCE

AS THE SPEAKER in the front of the room, you can engage your listeners through visuals, provocative questions, humor, vivid word choices, and stories. You can also invite them to participate with you individually, in smaller groups, or as an entire audience.

Keep in mind there will always be a small percentage of the population that does *not* want to play with you. I call these folks "curmudgeons" because they typically sit in the back and convey through their body language, "I don't want no stinking team activities!" In reality, however, once these folks get involved, real learning takes place. In order to make any of your activities work like a charm, follow these tips.

DEAL WITH OBJECTIONS. Anticipate why certain people might not want to participate. Address their objections ahead of time by saying something that makes it okay for them to get involved. For example, "I know some of you think these kinds of things are silly, but I promise there *is* a point, and it will only take a moment." Then let them participate to the extent they choose to. Even when they don't participate, they can still learn through observation.

SAVE FACE. Whatever you do, don't make anyone look stupid. Of course, the definition of "stupid" depends on the culture of the crowd, your topic, and your style.

INVITE. Watch your phrasing. Are you telling them what to do, or are you inviting them to participate? There is a *huge* distinction. "I want you to" evokes a different reaction from introductions such as "I invite you to" or "May I suggest" or "How about."

TRUST THE PROCESS. Let the group go through the process in their own way. Intervene only if you are running out of time or they are struggling. But if they are working *through* it, let it go! You'll be amazed at the number of times people say "Aha!" (as you will if you're open to it).

HAVE FUN. Go into each activity expecting people to love it. When you are enjoying yourself, others will too.

PROVIDE DIRECTIONS. If the instructions involve more than three things to do, not only explain the directions but also have them written down, either on the handout, on an easel chart, or on a slide for all to see.

KEEP THE ENERGY UP. Audience involvement usually creates a spike in energy. Consider what will be going on during any "downtime" in the activity. You don't want to lose the audience's interest.

DO A DRY RUN. Before asking the entire room to perform a specific activity, think it through carefully. Do at least one dry run all the way through before you attempt to do it with a live audience. If you have time, rehearse the activity multiple times during which you simulate different kinds of responses.

ATTRIBUTE. If you are using an activity taken from another source, get permission to use it and acknowledge that source. When in doubt, leave it out!

TASK INDIVIDUALS ⚠ ⚠

As you review your presentation, ask yourself whether you are doing something that an audience member could do just as easily. Contrary to popular belief, you do *not* need to do it all. Think through all of the elements of your speech and ask: "Do I really have to do this? Is there a way I can get an audience member or two/three/four involved?" When you ask an audience member to do something for you, she feels special. She morphs into a participant while sending a subliminal

GET YOUR AUDIENCE TO INTERACT

Amanda Gore, CSP, CPAE Speaker Hall of Fame

When I say, "Use audience interaction," I don't mean that you should ask a question and have them call out. You must go further. I have my audiences look at each other and *do* stuff! The more they connect, the better they can learn and actually have an experience (other than just listening to you or being entertained). Think of exercises to help them comprehend and remember the points you make.

signal to the rest of the audience that you are reaching out for help, and they might be more willing to cooperate when you ask them to do something later.

Here are some tasks that you can ask the audience to help you with.

LOGISTICS. Why not ask a participant to help you set up the room, hand out materials, or do whatever else you need to do either prior to your presentation or at a specific time during the presentation?

USHER. Ask the first people who arrive to kindly request that people sit toward the front of the room. This technique works well when you don't know how many people will be attending and the room has been set for possibly too many.

TIMEKEEPER. You can ask another person to be your timekeeper and let you know when you have five minutes, two minutes, one minute to go. Just be clear as to where this person should sit and what the cue will be. For example, it could be a certain number of fingers raised or a small sign or even having the person stand up.

RECORDER. Ask one or two people to help you write comments on an easel chart. Best to prepare them right before you begin your presentation because you will need to coordinate what the person will be writing and how you expect them to write it down.

COURIER. When materials need to be given to small groups, ask for one person from each group to come up to the front to get their materials.

RUNNER. If you will be using a sound system that allows participants to speak while they remain seated, then you may want to conscript a couple of people (one on each side of the room) to carry the cordless microphone to the participant who will be speaking. Coordinate details such as how you will identify who is next and whether or not you will let the participant hold the microphone. (There's something about holding a microphone, it seems, that compels people to go on longer than usual!)

HELPER. Ask one person to do something very specific for you. In my speech *Eight Hallmarks of a High Performing Team*, I find a friendly face a few minutes before the presentation and ask that individual to note how many times I use the words "I," "me," "mine," "you," "yours," "we," and "our." When we move into the section titled "Using Inclusive Language," the person stops and counts up the number of times I used these words. (To make things easier, I give him a tally sheet with these directions written on it.) A minute later, I ask him to share the numbers with the audience. I have just demonstrated my use of inclusive language (see chapter 1) and I always thank the person for his help.

VANNA. You can also ask a participant to act like Vanna White for you. Rather like Vanna turning the letters on the *Wheel of Fortune* game on television, your volunteer can hold a key prop for all the audience to see.

If your volunteer will need to read or prepare something ahead of time, give it to that individual well before your presentation starts so she can be comfortable with it. If the assignment involves color choices, make sure your volunteer isn't color blind!

WRITE IT DOWN ⚠

I am going to make the assumption that you have something in your speech that is worthy of writing down on a piece of paper and saving. Better yet, that the audience has something worthy of writing down to give to *you*! Let's look at several ways to be sure you collect those spontaneous gems.

TAKE NOTES. Encourage the audience to take notes, since it helps with learning and retention. When you are about to share the most important part of your presentation, encourage the audience to "Write this down."

PARK IT. Invite participants to write their question or idea or response on a sticky note or index card and post it on an area of your easel chart labeled "Parking Lot." If you use this technique, you *must* come back to the parking lot and deal with the sticky notes—even if it is simply to e-mail the contents of all those sticky notes and the answers to the meeting planner, who will forward them to all the attendees.

MAKE A LIST. People like lists. If you tell them you are going to list the three tips to try, the five footpaths to fortune, or the seven strategies to success, they will lean forward immediately and start taking notes. (Warning: Don't hand out the entire list at the start. You risk losing the audience's attention. If you hand out the list, either leave spaces where they will have to fill in the blanks or assure them they will have it as a takeaway after your presentation.)

QUIZ. Take a look at any mainstream magazine and you'll find one or two quizzes. People like short questionnaires that reveal insights about themselves and others. Just remember, if you ask the audience to invest their time filling out your questionnaire, you must provide the answers as well as how their answers compare to the answers of everyone else who has taken the test.

ASSIGN HOMEWORK. When appropriate, ask the audience to complete an assignment prior to your presentation. Make it a reasonable request that you believe a large percentage of the population will actually complete. Otherwise, don't bother to give them homework.

GAMES, PUZZLES, AND COMPETITIONS ▲ ▲ ▲

GAMES

Games are an energizing technique to get the audience involved as long as they are related to your topic and personalized as much as possible for your audience. There are a gazillion books out there that describe games and puzzles that might be suitable for your topic. I have suggested several books from my library in the recommended resources at the back of the book. 🔎 Or you can create your own unique activity.

GAMES TO REINFORCE YOUR POINT

Ed Scannell, CMP, CSP, author of the *Games Trainers Play* series

When using a game or participative activity, always be certain to identify the purpose or objective of the activity and allow time after to debrief and process the learning points brought forth. Time is all too precious to be "playing games," and unless your attendees understand and acknowledge why that particular exercise was used, that time is wasted and the program suffers. And remember—the game is an added reinforcement or embellishment to the content you're presenting. It is NOT the focal point! It can never be a case of the "tail wagging the dog"! But used properly, games will clearly make your program or presentation that much more meaningful and memorable.

PUZZLES

A puzzle is a specific type of game designed to challenge or test the audience's knowledge, ingenuity, or creativity. Most audiences are familiar with crossword puzzles, Sudoku, and wuzzles—a word puzzle that conveys an expression through an interesting display of words, numbers, and graphics. (Most people will have seen these in the *Parade* supplement in the Sunday edition of their city newspaper. The object is to try to figure out the well-known saying, person, place, or thing that each wuzzle is meant to represent.) These kinds of puzzles are great energizers at the start of the session, after returning from a break, or as a way to review the presentation. Try this wuzzle:

READING

COMPETITIONS

When it comes to setting up a friendly competition, you can take a popular TV game show or board game and adapt it for your presentation. *Who Wants to Be a Millionaire, Jeopardy*, and a version of Monopoly are common examples of games that lend themselves to audience participation. 🔍

INVENTING GAMES THAT GRAB THE AUDIENCE

Brian Walter, CSP

What audiences want are surprises, true participation, a little risk, and enjoying someone else's quasi-misfortune. That's the Audience Way—vicarious pain. In a speech or presentation, the most compelling way to drive up this exact kind of engagement is an audience competition where being wrong in front of everyone is a distinct possibility.

Our culture is rife with competition. That's what the masses in our culture (and in your audiences) clearly want. Need proof? *American Idol, Project Runway, Make Me*

Answer: reading between the lines.

a Supermodel, Celebrity Apprentice, Survivor, Iron Chef, and my personal favorite, *Dance Your Ass Off.* The top shows are all about competition. That's because competition is real. People are actually *doing* things. And they are being judged. Winners and losers. Drama.

So, when you tap into this aspect of popular culture and provide some actual competition in your presentations, you are creating an emotionally satisfying and memorable experience. That will make your content stick like a barnacle.

"But wait a sec" (you say), "I can't tell an audience member to pack up their knives and go home like on *Top Chef.* I'd be fired." You are right. In the workplace, your competition rules are different.

DEFINE THE RULES UPFRONT

Don't ask for volunteers before the audience knows what the competition is. Frame your request like this. "We are now going to play a game of nontrivial trivia about _____ . I will be asking ten multiple-choice questions and one triple point finale question. We need three brave contestants." See? In about ten seconds the audience knows what the story is. Now they are deciding whether they want to take the risk of playing. Most won't, but they like the idea of others playing and risking.

BRIBE FOR VOLUNTEERS

If you pick contestants, there's a limit on what you can ask them to do. They didn't ask to risk being wrong in front of their peers. So, if you pick people, you have to make the risk factor low. But low risk is boring. The way around all that is volunteers. You bribe them. "I need three volunteers who are willing to get up in front of everyone here and compete against their peers in an elimination contest. Oh, the winner will get _____ ." The prize can be high value (like a $50 Starbucks card) or humorously low value. "The winner will be competing for company logo'd items . . .with our old logo. Like a sweatshirt in any size you want, as long as it's XL." The entire audience will laugh at this. But you *will get* volunteers. They either want the prize or they want the attention. Regardless, they are willing to take a risk to get what they want. And by volunteering, they are psychically giving you permission to ask them questions they could get wrong.

MESS WITH THE RULES

To up the stakes (i.e., create more drama) you mess with the rules. After the first two questions or stages of your competition, you purposely break the rules. For example, if it's a multiple-choice question, the answer is "A" as well as "D." The contestants and the audience weren't expecting that. So, now they know that you are messing with their heads. It's a GOTCHA situation. They like that, and it also gives the contestants a break. They can get things wrong not because they don't know them but because you're asking trick questions. No one is actually sure what happens next. Surprise = drama.

CHEAT

Almost always, one of your contestants is going to freeze up. They will either get every question wrong or they will simply not "chime in" and play. To make this competition safer, you intervene—by cheating.

The most obvious way to is to give them the answer, but in a fun way. Let's say that you're doing a multiple-choice question and your contestant answers with "A," but the correct response is "C." You jump in with: "So, you don't SEE yourself picking any other answer? That's the one that you SEE as correct?" The audience will realize what you're doing first, and titter away. Often it will take a moment for your contestant to pick this up. Then they go, "Oh . . . right . . . actually I meant C, final answer." You leap in with "CORRECT," and the audience cheers even louder. You've helped them, and you've entertained the audience. So, while this is a competition, no one is upset that you cheated. They like you and the game BETTER because you did.

Another way to cheat is to help out a contestant who isn't chiming in. You simply say: "And this next question is just for . . . Chuck. We're calling this the Chuck Round. Only Chuck gets to answer." If Chuck answers incorrectly, you double-cheat and give him hints until he gets it right.

SNAPPY NAME

Your competition will be a "big moment" in your presentation. You can increase the impact of this competition by giving it a snappy name. Examples I use frequently include Brand Shout Out, What's Your Profit IQ?, Stay or Go, Yup or Nope, etc. Other speakers following you (often execs with your company or the client's company) will call back your memorable phrase or name from the game when communicating their content.

DEMONSTRATIONS ⚠ ⚠ ⚠ ⚠

It is one thing to talk about something in the abstract. It's quite another to show the audience what you are talking about. Demonstrate the value of your idea right in the moment! A demonstration extends beyond what your audience can see or hear; you can have them taste, smell, or touch an object, prop, or model. Whatever your topic, ask yourself these two questions: (1) Can I demonstrate "it" (or even a "bit" of "it") for the audience? and (2) Better yet, is there a way for the audience to experience it for themselves?

What follows is a list of methods you can use to demonstrate, not pontificate.

SHOW-AND-TELL. Think back to when you were in grade school and your teacher asked you to bring in an item of personal significance and tell a story about it. In your presentation, what can you show as you tell?

FOLLOW ALONG. Rather than demonstrate a thing, you can walk the audience through a process. Think of an episode of a cooking show in which they show you how to bake a cake. The first step is to assemble the ingredients; the second is to mix the ingredients together; and the third is to bake it. As you demonstrate your point, ask the audience to follow along.

DO AS I DO. For maximum involvement, take it to the next level and ask the audience to follow your lead. Show them something they can do while they are in the presentation room, and then have them do it. Though it is unlikely you will have each of them baking a cake in your presentation room, you could have them measure out the ingredients or some other piece of the process.

HOT SEAT. Take one volunteer from the audience to be coached by you—in front of the entire room. That's why it's called a "hot seat": all the focus is on the volunteer! You must be a master of your material for this method because you'll be using many of the same techniques when interviewing a participant. A word of caution is needed here. You cannot fake it through a hot seat. You must be present and totally focused on the volunteer and the audience—and be ready for just about anything.

FISHBOWL. When the group is too large to do the activity together, select some volunteers to do the activity while the others observe. This technique is known as the "fishbowl" because it is often done with the selected group working in a circle while the others in a larger circle around them observe the dynamics. It doesn't have to be in a fishbowl; for example, you can also have the smaller group in a line at the front of the room.

MAGIC TRICKS. Most people are amazed by magic, and you can hold the audience in the palm of your hand with an astounding magic trick. Unless you know a never-fail trick, or invest time and energy to learn one (there are lots of books on simple sleight of hand that might interest you), you might want to consider leaving your rabbit in the hat at home. 🔍

SKITS AND ROLE-PLAYS ⚠ ⚠ ⚠ ⚠

A more elaborate way to involve the audience is through skits and role-plays in which people in the audience act out assigned parts.

As with any stage production, the key to success is in the preparation. Be clear about the roles you and your volunteers will play, what you want them to do, and when they should do it. Think through how much will be "scripted" (hand them the words to say), improvised (give some general guidance), or completely spontaneous (no guidance given whatsoever).

Unfortunately, many audiences groan as soon as you use the term "role-play"—even though it is a very effective way to involve the audience and help them retain what they're learning. So, don't use this term. Call it an "activity." By the time they figure it out, they'll be knee-deep in the role-play!

GROUPS OF THREE. While there are many variations to role-playing, the most typical scenario involves dividing the audience into groups of three.

1. Role definition. Two participants are given the roles and a specific scenario (verbally and/or written) and one person or the entire audience observes the interaction.

2. Play. The two actors play out the scenario with the observer watching.

3. Self-critique. The actors comment on what worked and what didn't.

4. Observer critique. The observer comments.

5. Change roles and repeat above process.

SCRIPTED FISHBOWL. You can also script the role-play using just two volunteers. Prior to your presentation, select two "actors" who have enough time to familiarize themselves with the script. At the appropriate point in the program, ask the actors to come forward and play out the scenario and then have the audience observe and critique.

FISHBOWL. You can be more spontaneous when you put three to five chairs at the front of the room or in the middle (hence a "fishbowl" when everyone crowds around the chairs). Only the people sitting on the chairs in the middle are allowed to speak. If you have something to say, you sit on one of the central chairs. As long as you sit there, you can talk and discuss. If you have nothing to add, you go back to your place in the outer ring and let someone else take your place. If you are in the outer ring and have something to say, you tap the shoulder of one of the seated people who is not talking at that moment. That individual *has to* change places with you!

DEBATE. You can also set up a "debate" where opposing arguments are put forward. A typical "Point/Counterpoint" debate is when one side of the room prepares the "yes" argument and the other side of the room prepares the "no" argument to a specific question. For instance, make the statement, "To be a successful speaker, you must use humor." Have each side discuss their points and then create a process for each side to share their perspectives.

LINEUP. A shorter version of a debate is to dedicate one side of the room for one extreme opinion and the other side of the room for the opposite extreme. Ask the participants to choose one side or the other and to determine their place along the continuum by discussing the viewpoints of their fellow participants. This gets people moving and talking with each other.

Don't forget to check out more resources and downloads at www.boringtobravo.com.

CHAPTER ELEVEN RECAP

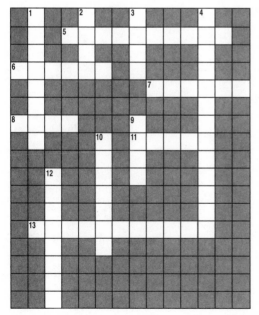

Across

5. 5-2-1 to go!
6. Point/counterpoint
7. Holds microphone
8. Monopoly is an example of one
11. Take your seats
13. Jeopardy

Down

1. Three-people scenario
2. As in shopping
3. Act a part
4. Show-and-tell
9. Short test
10. Get stuff
12. Write it down

Answer Key: *Across:* 5. Timekeeper; 6. Debate; 7. Runner; 8. Game; 11. Usher; 13. Competition *Down:* 1. Role-play; 2. List; 3. Skit; 4. Demonstration; 9. Quiz; 10. Courier; 12. Recorder

ACTION PLAN

Based on the information in this chapter, I intend to

Continue ⎯⎯⎯⎯⎯⎯⎯⎯⎯⎯⎯⎯⎯⎯⎯⎯⎯⎯⎯⎯⎯⎯⎯⎯⎯⎯⎯⎯⎯

Start ⎯⎯⎯⎯⎯⎯⎯⎯⎯⎯⎯⎯⎯⎯⎯⎯⎯⎯⎯⎯⎯⎯⎯⎯⎯⎯⎯⎯⎯⎯⎯

Stop ⎯⎯⎯⎯⎯⎯⎯⎯⎯⎯⎯⎯⎯⎯⎯⎯⎯⎯⎯⎯⎯⎯⎯⎯⎯⎯⎯⎯⎯⎯⎯

DYADS, TRIADS, QUADS, AND MORE

THE QUINTESSENTIAL GROUP INTERACTION is to break the large group into smaller discussion groups. It forces the participants not only to think about your message, but also to connect and collaborate with others and to apply the new information. It also inherently increases the energy level in the room!

Some people believe that these activities create downtime for the speaker. True, you may be able to take a moment to catch your breath and take a sip of water. But you are still working the room, monitoring what is going on, and bringing it all together for the debrief.

Whether it's sharing in pairs or a more complex activity, there are essentially six steps to every small-group activity:

1. Set up the activity.
2. Reflect.
3. Separate into smaller groups.
4. Give instructions.
5. Engage.
6. Debrief.

Depending on your objectives as well as your time constraints, you may opt to do all six steps or just a few. This chapter will take you through each one of the considerations for smaller group interactions.

STEP 1. SET UP THE ACTIVITY ⚠ ⚠

The old adage, "An ounce of prevention is worth a pound of cure," certainly applies when it comes to group activities. Since this is the most obvious form of group interaction, as well as one of the most significant investments of time, you need to be very clear about these key elements.

OBJECTIVE. Every group activity should be part of the program's objectives. If people cannot see immediate relevance (or they don't know you well enough to trust you), they will hesitate to play.

PROCESS. You should know the process you are going to use. Your process could include all six steps or be some variation.

ROLES. For larger group interactions, consider asking a few select participants to take on a specific task or role (see chapter 11). You may even assign a facilitator within the group to assist if the work is particularly complex or potentially volatile.

LOGISTICS. Have any necessary materials ready to use and on each group's table, or ask for a courier to come up to the front to get the materials. Steve Spangler, a celebrity teacher who frequently shares his science experiments on *The Ellen DeGeneres Show*, has a wildly fun group activity where people blow air through a "windbag." Since he does the activity at the conclusion of his presentation, he prearranges the neatly folded windbags on the table with a label around them that says "These are goodies for your after-lunch experience. While it might be tempting to play now, good things come to those who wait. —Thanks."

EASEL CHARTS. Some small-group activities include writing information on easel chart paper and then sharing that information with the larger group. You can post chart paper up on the walls ahead of time in the approximate location of each smaller group. Or write the small group topics on the easel charts as a teaser for what's to come!

INSTRUCTIONS. The larger the overall group, the clearer your instructions must be, and the simpler the logistics must be. Consider having the instructions written out (as part of your slide show, on an easel chart, or as a handout) as you set up the activity.

TEE UP. Tell the participants what you want them to think about or do—clearly, and with vigor!

STEP 2. REFLECT

Allow your audience a moment to think about the topic, question, or assignment. Encourage them to write their ideas down so that they are bringing their own unique perspective to the smaller group. Do you want their best idea? Ask them for it. The top three barriers to successful implementation? Ask them to write it down.

STEP 3. SEPARATE INTO SMALLER GROUPS

Separate the audience into pairs (dyads) or trios (triads) or foursomes (quads) or even more if necessary. Don't let the physical environment prevent you from small-group activity—just prepare for it!

The easiest way to separate a group into pairs or triads is to ask everyone to find a partner or to work with the people closest to them. If you had the audience pair up earlier in your presentation, ask them to search for a different person for a subsequent activity.

Want to put more energy into the room? Get a little creative!

FINGER. Ask the participants to stand up, put one finger in the air, search for someone they don't know, and touch finger to finger. Have pairs sit down next to each other close to the front of the room.

COMMONALITIES. Have participants find someone who has something in common with them (e.g., same color shoes or birthday in the same month/week).

MATCH CARDS. Take playing cards or postcards and cut them in half. Or make pairs of cards that have a word, phrase, or image on them. The pairs can also be synonyms and antonyms, famous couples, a famous quote and its originator, or a key word for the organization and a definition of that key word. Ask the participants to find the match to what's written/drawn on their card.

MUSIC. This is a variation on musical chairs. Ask the participants to walk around while loud, upbeat music plays. Let them know that their partner will be the person nearest to them when the music stops.

MERGE. The easiest way to move a group into a foursome is to merge two dyads into a quad.

PRE-SEATING. Seat the groups by tables or by rows before your presentation begins.

COUNT OFF. Count the total number of people you have (N). Identify the number of people you want in each group (P). Divide N by P and you have the number of groups you want (X). Then count off from "number one" through "X" around the room. Ask the audience to reorient itself so that each participant sits with the others having the same number.

CLUSTERS. Have everyone stand and form clusters of X number of people. You can give additional instructions, such as that each person in the group must be from a different table/company division/function.

DIVIDE. Set off the room areas by halves, corners, or seating sections.

PRESELECT. Preassign a number, letter, or color to each person on the nametags or name tents. When you need to break an audience into groups, ask for all the As to join together, all the Bs, etc.

SELF-SELECT. If everyone's working on the same issue, ask people to move into groups of no more than X number of people. If people will be working on different issues, post each issue on an easel chart and ask each audience member to move to the easel chart that interests them the most. (Note: you may have to do a bit of shuffling to balance the teams.)

PRESORTED TOYS. Place small toys on each table so that there is one for each person. Vary the toys so that they can be easily sorted. For example:

- Small stuffed balls—football, soccer, basketball, hacky sack, etc.
- Koosh balls—different colors
- Duplos® or Legos®—different colors and different sizes

Ask each person to select a toy and then have everybody with that particular toy regroup at the tables for a given activity. 🔍

PHYSICAL CHARACTERISTICS. Observe obvious physical characteristics that would allow you to break people into small groups. (Caution: make sure you won't offend anyone!) For example:

- Clothing—people wearing blue shirts/blouses/sweaters, brown, light-colored, etc.
- Gender—male, female
- Shoes—people wearing tennis shoes, sandals, oxfords, etc.
- Hair length—short, medium, long
- Pierced ears—those with and those without

STRATIFY. Separate the team based on some functional characteristic. For example:

- Geography—where people live or work
- Work unit—by unit, department, division, organization, company, etc.
- Position—by grade level within the company, such as employee, supervisor, manager, executive, etc.
- Age—Baby Boomers, Gen Xers, etc.

CONNECT THE LOST SOULS

Chris Clarke-Epstein, CSP

Pay attention to where you are standing as people are pairing up. Make sure your position gives you as wide a view of the room as possible. As people are getting into their groups, your job is to wander around or watch for those who look like they're having difficulty connecting. When you find a lost soul, you can lead them to a group and do the connecting. Or, suggest to the participants that they look around and see if there's anyone nearby who needs to be included.

STEP 4. GIVE INSTRUCTIONS ⚠ ⚠

Once people have settled into their small groups, give them all of the directions verbally. If there are more than three steps for them to remember, it's a good idea to supplement your instructions with a handout or by using a slide projected on the screen for all to see.

When handing out the instructions, either give them only to the group leaders—who then read the assigned activity, directions, or discussion questions aloud—or provide each person with a handout so the whole group can follow along as the activity is covered. There is no right or wrong here; it is simply a choice you should make.

Clarify instructions, if necessary, but don't let yourself get sucked into group discussions or debates—even if the group seems "stuck" or divided about which approach to take. Remember, the emphasis with this approach is on giving your participants experiences that will enable them to apply the content back on the job where you are not available to solve every problem or answer every question.

If you decide to assign such roles as "leader" or "spokesperson," help the audience select one using these methods:

- Close to. Individual with last name closest to the end of the alphabet or the person with birthday closest to the date you're making the presentation.

- Bait and switch. Say: "I'd like one person from each table to volunteer to do something. Once you've volunteered, I'll tell you what you're going to do." After you have one volunteer from each table, say "Great, you've just volunteered to help me find the first group leaders. They're the people seated to the left of every volunteer!"

- Finger in the air. Announce to everyone, "At the count of three, point to the person at your table who should be the leader." The person with the most fingers pointing at him or her leads.

- Most/fewest. The person with the most (or fewest) letters in his or her first name (or nickname or last name).

Be sure to confirm everyone's understanding. Ask if there are any last-minute questions before you invite them to play. Also be clear about your expectations, the sub-team's deliverable, the time frame, and, if necessary, the process they should follow. Then, let 'em go for it!

STEP 5. ENGAGE

Now is *not* the time to put your feet up and relax! Your work in this step is just as important as the rest of the speech because you are the eyes and ears for the audience.

ROAM. Wander around the room to watch and listen to people during small group activities.

BE ACCESSIBLE. Be available in case someone has a question.

EAVESDROP. Listen to what people are saying in their small groups. You may be able to incorporate this information into your debriefing. If you happen to hear a good comment or question, let the person know you would like everyone to hear what was said when you reconvene the whole group.

WARN 'EM! Give them a one-minute or thirty-second warning so they can finish their conversations.

BRING 'EM BACK. Quickly refocus the smaller groups and get them back into the larger group discussion.

- Acknowledgment. "I invite you to take your seats," "Thank you for being seated," or "You might not be completely finished, but that's okay . . ." works well for smaller audiences.

- Shush. Let out a long, drawn out "shush," just like you heard your teachers use in grade school.

- Clap. "Everyone who can hear my voice, clap your hands once." Then clap your hands once. A few people will clap their hands once. Then say, "Everyone who can hear my voice, clap your hands twice." Then clap your hands twice. Then continue three or possibly four times. By that point, you will have their attention.

- Rhythm. Teach the participants a rhythmic pattern of claps, finger snaps, and stomps that they will repeat whenever time is up.

- Lights. Blink the house lights on and off as they do in a theater.

- Noisemakers. Sound a noisemaker such as a Tibetan bell, cymbals, chimes, a singing bowl, a tuning fork, a kazoo, or a duck or train whistle to get their attention. 🔍

- Music. Play music during the small group activity and either significantly raise or lower the volume to signify the need to end it.

- Countdown timer. Create your own slide show that projects a clock that changes time every minute. To make it even more interesting, add music or pictures of the participants. You can also download our fifteen-minute countdown timer at www.BoringToBravo.com. 🔍

STEP 6. DEBRIEF ⚠ ⚠ ⚠

Once the group comes back together, you can either move on with your speech or, if there was some discussion or learning involved, you may want to debrief the activity. In essence, a debriefing session is a conversation about what happened during the small group activity and how it relates to your topic. The amount of time you devote to the debriefing depends largely on the complexity of and time involved in the activity and the importance of its outcomes to your point.

Here are the critical elements to include as you debrief any small group interaction.

THANK 'EM. Don't forget to thank everyone who participated in the small group activity.

FOCUS ON THE BIG PICTURE. Debrief the activity with key questions you prepared in advance. Go from general to specific:

- What just happened?
- What did you experience?
- How did you feel when . . .?
- What behaviors hindered/helped your progress?
- What surprised you?
- What was this activity designed to teach us?
- What happened here that you could use back on the job/in the real world?
- What are you going to do with this information?
- What's the one thing that sticks with you from this session so far?
- What are you going to do differently as a result of this session?

ASK FOR REPORTS. Ask individuals or the group leader to succinctly summarize—in less than one minute—the conclusions or best points of discussion of each group. Encourage them to stand and address the whole audience. When the number of small groups prohibits having every group leader give such a report, ask three group leaders for their summaries, and when those are given, encourage other leaders to give their reports by asking, "Do you have anything to add to what's already been said?" Conclude each report with a simple phrase of thanks.

EMPHASIZE. If you heard a great idea from a small group that you haven't heard in the reports and you want to bring it up, you might turn to the audience and say, "As I was wandering around, I heard XYZ, and I was wondering if others had the same thought . . ."

APPLY. Query whether the audience can apply a particular concept or idea to their own lives, businesses, or organizations.

REINFORCE. To underscore key learning points as they come up in the debriefing, add a little extra spin, some clarification, or a quick story if the audience needs it.

SUMMARIZE. Let the audience summarize by putting this question to them: "What are the key points we just experienced?"

ADAPTING TO LARGE AUDIENCES

Many presentations in the corporate world are given to groups of fifty people or fewer. You can make a meaningful connection with an audience that size by using the same techniques that are effective with groups of twelve to fifteen people.

But what if you want to engage an audience larger than fifty people? Can an audience of a hundred or more engage in a meaningful interaction? Contrary to popular belief, it can be done. I have spoken to groups with as many as two thousand people and used every major technique in this book. You *can* be interactive with larger crowds; you just need to adapt your activities to accommodate so many and to adjust the timing accordingly. Keep in mind the following ideas as you plan for large-group interaction.

EXPECTATIONS. Larger audiences tend to expect more formal presentations during which they will be passively informed and potentially entertained. Of course, it doesn't have to be this way, but you will need to set the tone as early as you can.

PURPOSE. Interaction for the sake of interaction makes the audience feel as if you are wasting their time. That effect is compounded in a large group. It is bad enough to have 10 to 15 people thinking that their time is being wasted; imagine the impact of 1,500 people feeling that way! For larger groups, you must be highly intentional about the purpose of using interactive techniques to supplement and support your key points.

TIMING. The larger the group, the longer it takes to get into and process an activity or interaction. Something that might take three minutes in a group of 15 could take six minutes in a group of 600. While there isn't a rule of thumb as to how much longer it will take, you need to factor in additional time for the audience to move, start the activity, actually perform the activity, and regroup.

ROOM SIZE. Larger audiences bring larger rooms and typically a theater-style setup, neither of which is exactly conducive to conversations. To make the setting more intimate, make sure the room is appropriate to the number of attendees. Take away empty chairs to force the participants to sit closer together. Set the room with round tables if possible. Make sure there are access lanes and spaces on the sides and along the back so that participants are able to move around.

SEPARATION. You will probably be on a platform, which inherently separates you from the crowd on the floor. Even though you want to be on the floor with them, it is not fair to the people in the back. So, if you want to move into the audience, do so with purpose and then get back up on the platform so all can see you.

EYE CONTACT. You may not be able to maintain eye contact with each individual, but you can mentally divide the room into sections and try to look out to all those areas equally.

GESTURES. You need to exaggerate your movements so all can see them as the audience size increases. For audiences with more than two hundred people, consider using an image magnification (IMAG) screen to make it easier for participants to see you. If you can afford it, have an extra camera to capture the image of audience members who are participating.

VOICE PROJECTION. The importance of managing sound increases exponentially with the size of the audience. It doesn't matter how loudly you speak; their experience is enhanced when audience members do not have to strain to hear you. Although I prefer using a microphone for any group larger than fifty people, a microphone is a *must* once you hit seventy-five or more people. Remember, it takes a moment for sound to travel—especially to the back of a long, narrow room. So it may take a moment for the audience to actually hear what you are saying, and then for their response to make it back up to you. If you have planned to interact extensively with the audience, have runners available with microphones or use stationary microphones set for audience members to use when speaking to you.

AUDIENCE PARTICIPATION. There is anonymity in larger groups, and they will remain individuals until you create a bond among them. As a general rule, the larger the group, the harder it is to get individuals to volunteer, so you need to carefully think through how you are going to select individuals to participate and whether you choose to reward them. Additionally, most audience members will participate in much smaller groups even though they are reluctant to speak up in the larger body, so think small, bite-sized activities that connect the audience not only to you, but to each other.

DYADS, TRIADS, QUADS

A LARGE GROUP INTERACTION

Randy Pennington, CSP, CPAE Speaker Hall of Fame

An international manufacturing company wanted to add meaningful participation and interaction to its 2-day meeting for 800 managers. The result was an experience that successfully addressed all of the factors listed above. Here is how it was done:

Room size and set: A round, rotating stage in the middle of the room created a more intimate feeling and decreased the feeling of separation. No one was more than 12 rows from the stage.

Visibility: The stage made one complete rotation every 15 minutes. That is slow enough to minimize disruption for the presenters and fast enough that everyone had a chance to maintain eye contact. In addition, IMAG screens set in the back corners of the meeting room displayed the images from four video cameras around the stage. This allowed everyone to see the presenters at all times. In addition, the cameras could swivel to pick up audience members who were speaking when not focused on the main presenter.

Voice Projection: Every participant used a wireless microphone to allow for movement on the rotating stage. In addition, four lighted microphone stations allowed audience member comments to be seen and heard. In addition, four "runners" with microphones supported spontaneous interaction.

Group Dynamics: Small group interaction created an opportunity for audience members to bond in a less intimidating environment. The traditional "stand up and go through the PowerPoint slides" presentations were replaced with interactive discussions where I acted as a facilitator with company executives. In addition, an audience response system (ARS) was utilized for specific sessions within the meeting to gather real-time feedback.

The result was an interactive and informative 2-day meeting that left participants feeling energized and engaged rather than bored and uninspired.

🔎 Don't forget to check out more resources and downloads at www.boringtobravo.com.

......

CHAPTER TWELVE RECAP

SMALL GROUP PROCESS CHECKLIST

1. Set up the activity
2. Reflect
3. Separate into smaller groups
4. Give instructions
5. Engage
6. Debrief

LARGE GROUP PROCESS CHECKLIST

- Expectations
- Purpose
- Timing
- Room size
- Separation
- Gestures
- Voice projection
- Audience participation

ACTION PLAN

Based on the information in this chapter, I intend to

Continue _____

Start _____

Stop _____

WHEN PRESENTING BECOMES FACILITATING

A COLLEAGUE OF MINE was asked to give a presentation. As he was doing his research, he discovered that the client wanted more than information delivered as a presentation; he wanted the participants to identify the issues, wrestle them to the ground, and figure out how to apply their outcomes to their organization.

As you involve the audience even more, you may find your role transitioning from presenting information to *facilitating* discussions among the participants as well. Extending beyond a few small group activities, the entire session becomes *one* large group interaction. The facilitator focuses on the *process* of the session (the how), rather than the *content* (what the topic is), enabling a group to move from the current reality to the desired outcome.

Be warned, however. Facilitation is not for the faint of heart. A process facilitator fundamentally believes that knowledge is resident in the room rather than in the mind of the speaker on the stage. A process facilitator literally makes things easier for the audience by enabling them to fully participate and collaborate. In its highest form, facilitation expects the participants to drive the agenda and the facilitator to guide them to achieve their objective. If you cannot give up the control of the content, facilitation is not for you.

Facilitation requires a tremendous amount of trust in the process you create to enable the group to move forward and in the group to be able to figure out what they need to hear, say, and do. Facilitation also usually takes more time than a more conventional presentation as the group members tackle their own understanding of the topic.

THE FACILITATOR

An effective process facilitator typically knows how to:

GUIDE THE PROCESS. As the process expert, you provide structure and process tools to help the group achieve its goal. At the beginning of your session, ensure the participants agree to the agenda and time limits. Keep the session on topic and moving along.

ENSURE A SAFE ENVIRONMENT. In the planning phase, think through the barriers to effective participation and ensure the environment is conducive to collaboration.

TEE UP THE DISCUSSION. You open up the discussion, setting the context or goal and sharing how the group will achieve the objective.

MANAGE PARTICIPATION. Once the discussion has been opened, you invite participation, manage the conversation flow, and tactfully prevent anyone from being overlooked or dominating the discussion.

MANAGE CONFLICT CONSTRUCTIVELY. Every group will experience some degree of conflict. Disagreements are natural and a normal part of the process. An effective facilitator makes sure the conflict is managed constructively to generate light around the issue and not heat.

CHECK DECISIONS. Groups make small decisions throughout a session. When you sense a decision has been made, check for understanding and agreement. Make sure the group understands the next steps and who will do them.

SUMMARIZE. When the conversation is finished or time runs out, you summarize the discussion based on what you heard. Confirm mutual understanding before you move on.

FROM PRESENTING TO FACILITATING

Joseph Sherren, CSP, HoF Speaker Hall of Fame

It was 1980 and my co-presenter, John, and I were just about ready to start a four-day leadership-training program for thirty-five IBM managers in Vancouver, British Columbia. John, who normally brings the overhead transparencies, turned to me and asked for the slides.

"I don't have them," I said casually. "You always have them."

John took a deep breath and sternly replied, "Last week, in our office in Toronto, you agreed to pick up the slides from Janette since you were going to be meeting with her anyway."

Oops. He was right. I forgot the slides.

We didn't have PowerPoint or overnight mail back then, so we had to figure out what to do—and quickly! After the appropriate introductions, I said to the group: "We have a special treat for you this week. John and I know that as a group of managers, you come to these workshops and are presented with a multitude of slides. So this time, we thought we would try something different. We will not be showing any slides. No, not one!" We got a standing ovation right at the start!

I then listed the different topics we would be addressing each day on an easel chart. Instead of making a presentation, we went around the room so people could share their best practices and other material from their experiences that had worked. At the end of each category, we followed up with any bits and pieces we needed to add.

We couldn't believe the response. For four days, the entire room was completely engaged, and that program was the best-rated program for the year. Participants were raving about the lessons learned for years afterward. But it wasn't just a one-way street. We discovered we didn't have all the answers either. We learned some new techniques and best practices from the participants as well.

Necessity is the mother of invention, and we learned to be the guides and facilitators of learning rather than the wise speakers with dozens of slides the participants were compelled to sit, read, and absorb.

FACILITATION

CLARIFY NEXT STEPS. Every session should end with specific tasks assigned to specific participants. Otherwise, you have just had a great conversation, but no results! Ensure all understand who is responsible for what and by when.

INTERVENE. When the group gets off track or if the discussion fragments into multiple conversations, you step in to bring the group back on topic.

Many facilitation skills are similar to those contained in this book; however, there are additional process skills that you need in addition to your presentation skills.

DEVELOP A PROCESS AGENDA

Typically, a facilitated session is one meeting among a series of meetings. As a facilitator, one of your first challenges is to clarify the session objective as well as the overarching goal for the series of meetings. You will still do some research on your audience, but clarifying the objective is typically done in collaboration with the meeting planner or other interested stakeholders in the success of the event.

Based on the clarified objective, you build the meeting agenda. A basic agenda is similar to a presenter's outline; however, the focus is more on the topics for discussion rather than topics to be presented. A typical agenda consists of some opening activities, topical discussions, and closing activities:

1. Open the meeting
   - Establish/review agenda
   - Icebreaker activity
2. Topic #1
   - Introduce topic
   - Discuss
3. Topic #2
   - Introduce topic
   - Discuss

4. Close the meeting

- Summarize key understandings and next steps
- Critique

Think through the process thoroughly. What can you have the participants do? If you need to keep time (I am *terrible* at keeping time!), have a participant keep time for you. If you need to record ideas on an easel chart, assign a participant to be your recorder. If you need to introduce a topic, ask an expert to do so. Whatever you decide to do, prepare for it. And remember, facilitated sessions generally take more time because the agenda and process are customized uniquely for the topic and the group.

HOW TO BUILD AN AGENDA FROM SCRATCH

If an agenda has not been developed before the session, you can let the group create its own in the first five or ten minutes of the meeting. Quickly hop up out of your seat, grab a chart marker, and do the following:

- ◆ Ask, "What do we need to accomplish at this meeting?"

- ◆ Write down each idea the way it was stated and the name of the person who suggested the idea. Note: You are asking the team to identify outcomes or expected results, not just a list of topics.

- ◆ Ask if everyone understands the outcomes and clarify if necessary.

- ◆ Combine similar items. Should there be any dissent, assume that the ideas are distinct and should remain separate.

- ◆ Take each item and ask the person who suggested it how long it will take to achieve the outcome. If the group disagrees, allow a few seconds for discussion and write down the most agreed-upon time. Remember: an agenda is just a road map and the time limits are simply guideposts. If the group later agrees that it needs more time, you will have the flexibility to adjust the agenda.

FACILITATION

- ◆ Ask the people who suggested items if they would like to lead the discussion. If they decline, ask the group for a volunteer. Beware: avoid asking one or two people only to lead the items; otherwise, you'll end up with a one-way conversation!

- ◆ Prioritize your list. Most groups have too much to do and not enough time, so it is critical to start with the most important. Some groups simply rank the agenda items by number, starting with one as the most important, two as the next most important, etc. For a variation, try the ABC concept:

  - ◆ "A" is vital—We must accomplish this outcome at this meeting.

  - ◆ "B" is important—We should try to accomplish this outcome.

  - ◆ "C" is trivial—We could do this, but the world won't come to an end if we don't accomplish this today.

When prioritizing, quickly go through the list and ask, "Is this an A, B, or C?" and write down the most agreed-upon letter.

Optional: Continue to prioritize by sequencing each item assigned to the letters: for example, identify A1, A2, A3, B1, B2, B3, and so on.

You have now built your agenda! Start with the A1, and move through the list. It will take no more than ten minutes for such a worthwhile investment in the group's buy-in and accomplishments.

GODA PROCESS FLOW

At a macro level, all group conversations start with a free-flowing discussion that generates ideas, problems, causes, solutions, etc. Most of you have participated in some variation of a brainstorming session at one time or another, but brainstorming doesn't stop once you generate a list of possibilities! From the list, the group must somehow organize the possibilities in order to make a decision. Once a decision has been made, the group needs to take action.

I call this the GODA process—generate, organize, decide, and act.

GENERATE YOUR LIST

Developed in the late 1930s by Alex F. Osborn to stimulate his advertising executives' creativity, brainstorming has blossomed across America's meeting rooms. You can also use this ubiquitous technique in your presentation to generate as many ideas about a subject as possible. The concept is about getting all of the ideas out on the table without evaluation or judgment. It's about quantity, not the quality of the ideas.

Although we assume most people are familiar with the term "brainstorming," don't count on it. Before you begin, remind your audience of the simple ground rules:

- All ideas are valid.

- Any idea is acceptable, even if it seems silly, strange, or similar to a previous idea.

- Say "pass" if you don't have an idea on your turn.

A person will be assigned to quickly capture ideas on a piece of paper for two to four people, an easel chart for groups up to thirty people, and displayed electronically for larger groups so all can see. You are encouraged to add other ideas, otherwise known as "hitchhiking." The process continues until everyone passes (or a predetermined time limit runs out).

Remember: no praise, no comments, no criticism. It's brainstorming!

Three different methods are typically used to brainstorm a list:

1. Freewheel. Anyone on the team can call out an idea, with one person (presumably you, the speaker, but it doesn't have to be) capturing the ideas for all to see.

2. Round-robin. Go around the room so that each person has a chance to contribute a new idea, add to, or hitchhike on a previous idea. Each person has the option to pass. You can switch to freewheeling as more participants pass.

3. Slip. Encourage all of the participants to write down in large and legible letters each of their ideas on a separate slip of paper, sticky note, or index card. A great side benefit of writing each idea separately is that team members are expressing their ideas in their own words and in as much detail as they like.

ORGANIZE YOUR LIST

Once you finish your brainstorming session, you can organize ideas in one of three different ways:

1. Synthesize. You can summarize what has been said by synthesizing all the ideas into a handful of headlines or highlights.

2. Sort. You can have the group sort the ideas into a few manageable categories or in a specific flow, for example, chronological, process, along a continuum, and so forth.

3. Prioritize. You can have the group narrow down the pool of ideas into a smaller, prioritized list.

Let's look at option 2 in greater detail. To sort the brainstormed list, you can have the group categorize, affinitize, or flow their ideas.

CATEGORIZE

If they already have a sense of the general categories, then simply label each of several easel charts with the name of one of the chosen categories. Then ask the team members to place their sticky notes or index cards in the appropriate category. Leave one blank sheet of paper up on the wall just in case another category emerges. Make sure you have enough wall space for posting these ideas so that your team can sort through the ideas. You'll be amazed at how quickly the brainstormed list shifts from a huge blob into several discrete clusters.

HOW TO BRAINSTORM

1. Clarify the topic. Start your brainstorming session by clarifying the topic at hand. Write the topic on an easel chart or slide for all to see.

2. Review the ground rules.

3. Have each member offer an idea about the topic. Other members refrain from any comment, listen carefully, and build on one another's ideas.

4. Have the recorder write down all ideas so that all can see.

5. Continue until the group has exhausted its ideas on the topic or you have used the prescribed amount of time.

   ♦ Optional: Discuss ideas for clarification.

   ♦ Optional: Combine similar ideas, with the permission of the team.

6. Summarize key ideas and segue into the next step.

FACILITATION

AFFINITIZE

Sometimes, the team doesn't know what the main categories might be. In this case, ask the team to affinitize their ideas. In this process, place several sheets of blank easel chart paper on the wall. Then ask the team members to take each card and place it next to another card with a similar idea, an affinity, or something in common. If the idea is exactly the same, simply put your card on top of the other one. It's okay if you have a card that has nothing in common with the others; just put it on another place on the wall. Either other ideas will start to cluster around it, or it will remain an outlier.

FLOW

The ideas may need to be sorted along some specific criteria. For example, if the group is creating a timeline, they will sort the cards chronologically. If describing a process, they will sort the cards as the process currently operates. Here are the three steps to follow no matter what option you use:

1. Silent sort. The key to sorting the papers, sticky notes, or index cards quickly is to do so without talking. Once all of the ideas are up on the wall or on the table, they are now the team's ideas. If a team member doesn't like where an idea note or card has been placed, he or she can move it rather than discuss it.

2. Countdown. After the flurry of activity, give a ten-second countdown for all ideas to be settled into their clusters.

3. Confirm the clusters. Label each cluster with a header that describes all of the idea notes or cards in that cluster. Or, if the categories are predetermined, confirm that the category header still applies to all the notes underneath it.

Whether you categorize or affinitize your ideas, you get the same result—several categories or headers with several cards underneath each one. The advantage of using an affinity diagram is that you might see some nontraditional, even creative groupings of your ideas.

Now that you have organized that huge brainstorming list, your team may decide to prioritize the categories or headers to focus on one or two high-priority ones. Or your team may decide to divide into sub-teams to look at each category in more detail.

TAKE A QUICK VOTE OR MULTIVOTE TO PRIORITIZE YOUR LIST

Similar to taking a poll, the quick vote allows you to take a long list of possibilities and narrow it down by at least a half, if not two-thirds. It's analogous to shaking a bottle of oil and vinegar; when you put the bottle down to settle, the oil floats to the top. Your quick vote allows the items of most interest to rise to the top of the group's priority list.

The easiest and fastest way to get a quick vote is to ask the group, "Of all the things we have just considered, what is your top priority?" Then go around the room and capture their responses. Or, if the list is already posted on an easel chart, just put a check mark next to the item as each person votes. You will see a vibrant list of the top priorities emerge.

For a larger group with a larger list, you can also go through these five steps of casting multiple votes, also called a "multivote":

1. Clarify and combine. Before you move into a vote, ask if anyone needs clarification of an item, or if any two items are so similar they should be combined. If the majority of the group agrees, then combine them. If any one member loudly disagrees, keep them distinct.

2. Ten votes. Each participant has ten votes. They can place all ten votes on one item or they can scatter their ten votes among the many items. (If the list is more than thirty items, you may want to consider allowing the team members to have more votes—typically a third of the items. For example, if you have fifty-one items, then each team member would have seventeen votes. Notice that it will be a bit harder and longer to vote and tally—especially if you have lots of participants.)

3. Silently vote. Ask each participant to silently vote by writing item choices and the number of votes on a piece of paper. To speed up this process, you may want to letter each item, starting with A, then B, and so on down the chart. Then the team members simply write the letter and the number, for instance, A-3, F-2, H-2, I-2, and L-1. Ask the participants to make sure they have cast all of their ten votes.

4. Tally the votes. Go through the list, starting with A, and ask the participants to raise the number of fingers for the number of votes they placed on that item. The recorder may then simply count up the numbers, or

FACILITATION

the participants may choose to sound off in sequence by adding their numbers together. Write the total next to the item and take the vote on the next item until you have gone through all of the items.

Note: If privacy is an issue, ask the participants to write each of their items and the corresponding vote on small, separate sticky notes. For the previous example, the participant would have five separate notes. After the votes of all of the participants have been recorded, turn the easel charts out of sight of the team, and ask each individual to come up to the easel charts and place the sticky notes next to each item. Since this takes a bit longer, take a break after everyone has filed through and voted. The recorder simply pulls off the sticky notes from each item and adds them up. If a sticky note falls off the chart, it's easy to see where it belongs, since both the letter and the vote are written on the sticky note.

5. Shorten the list. After all votes have been registered, ask the group for the item with the highest number of votes, followed by the next, and the next, and so on. Capture the new list on an easel chart. You will see the list narrow down dramatically—at least by half.

There may be some vocal members who will want to take the top vote and declare it the winner. Be careful—less than 50 percent of the group may have voted for the winner!

The first round of voting is used to narrow down the list, not to select a winner. If your list is really long, you may even do a few multiple votes to narrow down the list to something manageable.

When you have narrowed the list down to five or so items, see if there is a possible consensus in the mix of ideas. Is it possible to combine or create, or must the team select just one?

EXPERIMENT: ORGANIZE YOUR IDEAS

At the next meeting you attend, watch how the group organizes their ideas. For example, they may come up with a simple list of potential action items. As the group goes through the list at the end of the meeting, does it get organized/sorted into a "do" or "do not" list?

DECIDE WHICH OF YOUR IDEAS TO PURSUE

Perhaps an obvious option leaps out of the pack and the group comes to a quick decision. Most of the time, however, they are faced with a choice among many options.

If the group is interested and has the time, it can combine, create, and synergize the items into a better idea. The group builds a consensus—striving to reach a decision that best reflects the thinking of all of the participants. Consensus means more than "I can live with it." It means that each person can live with *and* support the decision upon implementation. Here are steps you can take to build a consensus:

DEFINE "CONSENSUS." Explain what consensus means and why it is important for the group to reach a collaborative "win-win." Ensure that all participants understand the issue and the most important items. To prevent confusion, take the time to define the specific meaning of the words being used. Clearly outline any constraints (e.g., time or money). Remind each member to participate fully in the discussion, and that they have an equal voice. Finally, identify a fallback, majority vote, or command decision, if consensus can't be reached within a specified time.

ASK QUESTIONS. Take the most important items from your smaller list, category headers, or ideas within a category, and ask a few probing questions such as these:

- All of these items are possible. Do we have to choose only one?
- Is there any way we can use the best features of each item?

FACILITATION

- What would happen if we took the added/deleted features of several options? Would that get us closer to what we want?
- Could we try out several options in parallel before we commit to just one?

Team energy increases as new ideas and possibilities surface. This trial-and-error approach appears chaotic; however, the group builds a new, synergistic alternative based on the best of the best.

TAKE A STRAW POLL. When it appears the group has coalesced and agreed to a new alternative, take a straw poll, a pulse check to see how close or how far the team is from reaching a consensus. Remind the group that this poll is not a final vote; it simply tells them how much work needs to be done to build consensus. Use these sentences to help the group move forward:

- It sounds like we're making progress. Let's check that out with a quick straw poll to see how close we are to a consensus. We'll go right around the table. Sally?
- Let's see if everyone can either agree with or agree to support the most popular alternative. Let's start with Sally and go around the room.

Record the responses and summarize the results. If everyone can live with and support the alternative, then you have a consensus.

BUILD A BETTER DECISION. Chances are there will be some opposition, so find out what it would take to gain support. Try these simple questions to break a deadlock:

- There seems to be a lot of support for this alternative. What would it take for the rest of us to support this?
- What is getting in the way of some team members supporting this alternative? What could we do to meet their needs?

Continue to build agreement for the decision until you have a consensus, or time runs out and your team falls back to another decision-making method. By building a consensus, your group has a greater chance of producing a better quality decision, a more cohesive team, and smoother implementation of the decision.

THE 5L TEST FOR CONSENSUS

When it appears the team has coalesced around a decision, I like to do the 5L test for consensus before we actually ordain the decision:

1. Establish everyone's complete understanding of the straw poll issue. Clarify any lingering questions the group may have.

2. Give each participant one removable colored dot. You can also "stratify" the different members within the audience by giving different colored dots to distinct groups.

3. Draw the 5L scale on the easel chart. Walk through the definitions of each L and ask participants to silently vote on what they think of the solution:

   ♦ You Loathe it.
   ♦ You will Lament it and moan about it in the parking lot.
   ♦ You can Live with it.
   ♦ You Like it.
   ♦ You really Love it.

4. Ask the participants to place their colored dot on their reaction to the solution, so that they are building a bar chart.

5. After all of the group members have placed their dot on the chart, step back and evaluate. Based on the results of the straw poll, see if the group agrees there is consensus.

   ♦ Consensus is that all votes are at least a "live with" or better.

   ♦ If there are votes that are "loathe," "lament," or just a few "live with," ask the group why some of them voted that way. Be careful not to pick on a specific person, but get the group's feedback on why there isn't consensus.

   ♦ Integrate the new feedback and build a better solution.

FACILITATION

ACT ON YOUR IDEAS

A few years ago, I was asked to observe a CEO's meeting with his direct reports. They had a robust discussion about their website strategy. It appeared to me that they agreed to a handful of great ideas. After the meeting was over, I asked the CEO, "So, who is going to take action on these great ideas?" The CEO stared at me, believing that one of his VPs would pick up the ball. When I queried the VPs who were at the meeting, they each assumed someone else was going to take the lead. As a result, nothing got done—until the next meeting.

In the next chapter, I will share several proven techniques to make your presentations stick and do the same for facilitated sessions. In fact, accountability is even more important in a facilitated session because the group itself owns the result. If there is no action, the session is a waste of everyone's time.

RECORD POSSIBLE ACTIONS. The group has had a great conversation and made some decisions along the way. Have an easel chart ready to record ideas as they emerge as well as the name of the person who suggested the task.

REVIEW ACTIONS. Review the "action plan" at the end of the meeting. Make sure the group thoroughly understands the task assigned and the scope of the work. You may discover a task doesn't need to be done at all.

CONFIRM RESPONSIBILITY. Confirm the name of at least one person responsible for completing each task (always ask for volunteers first and suffer the silence). That person is accountable to the group for ensuring that the task will be completed. Notice that it doesn't mean they have to do all of the work, but they do have to marshal the right people and resources to get the job done.

CHECK FOR HELP. Ask the person responsible if they are going to need some help, and then quickly identify who will help them. It's a good practice for those people to touch base right after the meeting to set up a time to get together.

SET A SPECIFIC DUE DATE. Rather than writing down the vague note "next week," target a specific date and time: for example, February 11 at 10:00 a.m. By assigning a specific date, the task becomes much more tangible and can be written on each participant's calendar. If appropriate, put the task on a timeline and show how it affects other events or tasks.

DOCUMENT. Capture the action items in the meeting minutes. Typically, minutes are sent out within two days of the meeting as a quick reminder to each participant.

JUST DO IT. Once the commitment has been made, it is up to the individuals to do their fair share—and for the group to hold them accountable. As a facilitator, you have to set up the structures for this to happen.

🔍 Don't forget to check out more resources and downloads at www.boringtobravo.com.

CHAPTER THIRTEEN RECAP

Every group goes through a predictable pattern of discussion. As the facilitator, you can guide them through the GODA process:

FACILITATION

Generate	Quantity		
Organize	Sort		
	Prioritize		
Decide	Agree		
Act	Plan		

ACTION PLAN

Based on the information in this chapter, I intend to

Continue _____

Start _____

Stop _____

CHAPTER FOURTEEN

MAKE YOUR MESSAGE STICK

YOU CAN GIVE an engaging and interactive speech, but if you haven't inspired your audience to think, feel, or do something differently, you have wasted everyone's time. The brutal fact is that there is a gap between the cup and the lip. You have all this information brimming in your cup, so, what are you going to do to move the cup closer to their lips so they can drink?

REVIEW AND REVISIT ⚠

You can review your main points *or* you can have your audience revisit the program content. Ask them to share something they learned or felt; it can even be something they already knew that was reinforced or relearned with a new emphasis. In the recap and review at the end of each chapter, you've already seen the following list of review techniques you can use:

1. Review
2. Revisit
3. Memorable phrases
4. True or false?

5. Visual slides

6. Questions

7. Q&A

8. Summarize

9. Fill in the blank

10. Word match

11. Crossword puzzle

12. Checklist

13. Visuals

14. Write it down

15. Process flow diagram

16. Action plan

You can adapt these examples to fit your presentation; you can also choose from among these other techniques to revisit your main points:

- Shout out. Periodically ask your participants to shout out what they consider to be the most important point(s) made up to that point and how they can personally apply the information.

- Ask for examples. Interrupt your presentation periodically and ask participants to give examples of the concepts you've just presented.

- Integrate. Encourage your participants to think about the new information and how it fits with what they already know.

- Challenge. Take it one more step and ask, "So, what are you going to do about it?"

- Nudge your neighbor. Ask the audience members to talk with the person sitting to their left or right about the most meaningful point(s) made so far that are most applicable to their work, and how they will apply the information when they get back to their workplace.

CREATE A STRONG, COMPELLING CALL TO ACTION ⚠

This is the crucial point where the cup meets the lip. You can have a great speech, but if you haven't shifted the audience's perspective, increased their knowledge, or inspired them to do something differently, your words are for naught. Your audience will not take action unless you ask them to. Don't assume they know what they should do as a result of your brilliantly crafted speech. It might be something as simple as asking them to consider the new ideas. Or you may want them to implement the new ideas immediately! You need to top off your presentation with an explicit request, or you might ask the participants to create/share what they are going to do as a result of your speech.

> **EXPLICIT REQUEST.** Salespeople are always encouraged to "ask for the order." You should make a similar request of your audience. What do you want them to *do*? Suggest a relatively easy action they could do when they get back to their offices that day or the day after your presentation. Ask them to do that easy action or make a more challenging request.

> **DO IT NOW.** Get them to take the first step *in the room*. It might be something as simple as signing a form to express their interest.

> **RHETORICAL + DECLARATIVE.** With the rhetorical question, you are getting emotional agreement. The declarative allows the participants to recognize that real action can result. For example: "Can we do this? Yes, we can. We must do . . ."

> **REFLECTIONS.** At the beginning of your presentation, encourage participants to write their special ideas or revelations on a notepad, sticky note, or their handout as they listen and participate. Toward the end of your speech, create a quiet space during which your participants can review what they jotted down and reflect on what they heard and learned.

> **ACTION PLAN.** Ask the group to create their action plan, that is, meaningful next steps as a result of the program and key takeaways. Some closing questions include:

MAKE YOUR MESSAGE STICK

- What is the one thing that you want to change in the next three months as a result of the information you heard today?
- What are you going to do differently based on what you have learned?
- What three things are going to move you closer to your goal?
- What will your first action step be as a result of today's event? How will you reward yourself for completing this action?

CREATE ACCOUNTABILITY

You asked your audience to revisit the key messages and they identified a few meaningful steps forward. You can create an accountability structure that supports the participants' desire to follow up on their commitments. After all, how many times do we leave a presentation with good intentions and then get caught up in the urgencies of the day?

PUBLIC PROCLAMATION. Allow the opportunity for your participants to declare in front of their peers what they will do. You can do this with a show of hands or go around the room and ask, "What's the one thing you are committed to doing as a result of this presentation?" Once people make a public proclamation of their intent, there is a greater probability they'll complete it because they know that someone in that room might hold them accountable.

WRITE IT DOWN. Ask your audience to write their commitments on a blank 3 x 5 index card. You can preprint the cards with a specific call to action. For example, "Here are three things I will do to engage and interact with my audience."

ACCOUNTABILITY BUDDY. Ask the audience to find a partner (new or "used") with whom to share their commitment. It's best to have the group pair up in groups of two; possibly three, but no more. The buddies exchange written commitments and contact information (get those business cards ready!). They agree to touch base at an agreed-upon interval (once a week or once a month) until the item is completed.

Some of the ways you can encourage accountability buddies include the following:

- Ask participants to simply shake hands with a buddy, exchange business cards, and make a solemn vow to follow up in one month.

- Have everyone write his or her commitment on a preprinted index card and exchange it with the accountability buddy: "I promise to call (accountability partner) on (date) and report my progress on (key thing each will do as a result of the session)." Signatures and phone numbers go on the cards.

- Provide preprinted multi-copy forms on which the participants write down their action plan. They keep the original form, a copy can go to the buddy, and you can keep another copy to enable you follow up and to provide the meeting planner with your compiled results.

END WITH THE AUDIENCE IN MIND ⚠

You have taken your audience on a journey that was propelled by a conversation about where they were at that moment and where they were headed. As you conclude the presentation, end on a high note. Because the closing is the part that the audience remembers the most, make it strong and memorable.

SUMMARIZE. Quickly review your main points for your audience's benefit. For example, "Today we explored three important ideas about . . ."

GIVE FEEDBACK. If you were truly having a conversation with your audience, tell them what you heard them saying. For example, "Here are the three things I learned from all of you today . . ."

CONNECT WITH THE BEGINNING. Take a question you posed at the beginning and "close the loop."

USE A STORY. Tell a powerful and memorable story to illustrate what you heard.

END ON TIME. Early on in my career, I heard Ambassador Vernon Walters close his presentation with this safe advice: "I must go now while you still want me to stay." Even if they are hanging on your every word, do *not* go over time. Ever. It's about honoring your commitment to them, and going over time is the most obvious and easiest way to disengage them.

GIVE THEM A TAKEAWAY. Always leave them with something they'll remember you and your presentation by.

BE AVAILABLE. Your audience may want to continue the connection by sharing a story or offering some additional information in a less formal setting. Stick around. Listen to what they are telling you.

EXTEND THE CONVERSATION

You thought you were done with your presentation, didn't you? Well, you could consider your work to be done. On the other hand, you can extend your message beyond the actual presentation and encourage progress on the commitments made, by following some or all of these steps:

SEND A THANK-YOU. Send a note or an e-mail of appreciation to each person who was instrumental in the success of the presentation. Among these should be the decision maker who brought you in, the meeting planner who coordinated the details, and the A/V technician who wired you for sound.

KEEP YOUR PROMISES. If you promised to get the name of a great book, research the answer to a question, or send an interesting article or copies of your slide show, then do it as soon as you can after your speech.

PROACTIVELY CALL. Select a handful of participants (or all of them if the group is small enough) and call and ask them if they did what you asked them to do during your compelling call to action.

MAIL COMMITMENTS. If the group members wrote their commitments on 3 x 5 cards, ask them to self-address an envelope that you'll provide. Then mail their commitment card to each of them thirty days after your presentation.

As a result of what happened here today . . .what are you going to do about it?

(Write down the actions you are willing to take . . .)

Please write your name and mailing address on the envelope provided and seal it. I will mail this card to you in thirty days.

Yes! You CAN make a difference!

BE AVAILABLE. Offer to be available after the presentation for phone calls or e-mail within a prescribed period of time (a week is customary). Post your contact information on an easel chart, or slides, or in your handout or takeaway.

OFFER INDUCEMENTS. Make the point that you want to hear from the audience and offer a token of appreciation if they do.

SUMMARIZE. Review the important points of the speech in an article for the company newsletter, blog, or intranet.

TELECONFERENCE. Offer a followup teleconference exclusively for the attendees, including an invitation for them to submit questions or request amplification of ideas presented in the session.

MAKE YOUR MESSAGE STICK

RECOMMEND RESOURCES. You are one resource, but there may be other books, articles, websites, etc., that would be valuable resources to share with your audience. Send an e-mail with a list of additional resources.

ASK FOR E-MAIL. Ask the participants to send you an e-mail thirty days after the session with their answers to one or more of these questions:

• What did you try?
• How did you apply what you learned?
• What happened? What are your results?
• How did you revise your approach or changed your priorities as a result of the outcomes?
• What's something you are still wondering about?

To increase your response rate, you may want to offer some kind of incentive for sending the e-mail. Forward the collection of e-mail to the meeting planner and suggest that that person send the participants a note of congratulations for applying the techniques and being so well organized.

SEND AN E-MAIL. If you captured the group members' commitments, send an e-mail in which you repeat the commitment and ask a friendly, "How's it going?" Offer support and your assistance, if necessary. You can take the response data and feed this back to the meeting planner as well.

POST. Post information that supported your presentation (your slide show, relevant articles) on a designated website.

BLOG. Create a blog or chat board through which the attendees can continue the conversation. This is especially valuable in situations where the content of the speech provoked the need to seek more ideas or to share different perspectives.

SURVEY. Create a simple, Web-based survey to assess steps people have taken and the results they have achieved. 🔍

🔍 Don't forget to check out more resources and downloads at www.boringtobravo.com.

CHAPTER FOURTEEN RECAP

Write down three things you will do to encourage your audiences to take action.

1. _____

2. _____

3. _____

ACTION PLAN

Based on the information in this chapter, I intend to

Continue _____

Start _____

Stop _____

MAKE YOUR MESSAGE STICK

CHAPTER FIFTEEN

INFUSE YOUR PRESENTATION

NOW THAT YOU HAVE RIFFLED THROUGH all the myriad techniques to engage and involve your audience, you may be wondering just how you will make your current presentation or one that you are putting together more engaging and interactive

Let's assume that your presentation follows the familiar structure of an opening segment, three to five points, and a closing segment. You basically have two options from which to choose. And your choice depends completely on the time you have to prepare, the importance of the speech, and the "personality" of your audience. Your two options are these:

1. Peppering. For presentations you don't have a lot of time to prepare for, you can pepper an existing speech with some of these techniques. Go through the book and highlight those techniques that (1) will resonate with the specific audience you'll address, and (2) you authentically believe in and want to do. It's like taking a coat off the rack at a department store and trying it on for size. The moment you put it on, you know instinctively if you like it or not. And if you do, it probably will need some adjusting to fit you. The same is true about these techniques and your audience.

2. Infusion. You can infuse your presentation using a deliberate process I will share with you for the remainder of this chapter. Keep in mind that you may not need to do all eight steps, or you may choose to do all eight of the steps but with a tad less rigor than I am suggesting. That is perfectly okay; the extent to which you use this process will depend on a number of factors, among them the audience's personality, the energy in the room, your objectives, and so on.

HOW TO INFUSE YOUR PRESENTATIONS

The eight steps for infusing your presentation with engaging and interactive techniques are:

1. Do your homework about the audience.

2. Lay out your presentation in bits.

3. Identify your objective(s) for each bit.

4. Note the current techniques.

5. Lay out the energy curves.

6. Brainstorm different techniques.

7. Select the most appropriate technique.

8. Do a dry run.

Let's look at each step in greater detail.

STEP 1. DO YOUR HOMEWORK ABOUT THE AUDIENCE

An engaging presentation is all about your audience. So, if you don't know them already, do your research so you can infuse your presentation with techniques that will resonate with that specific group. Even if you do know them well, learn all you can about who will be in the room through interviews with the meeting planner, selected participants, or other people in the know.

HISTORY. Discover what worked well with the audience in the past so you can build on their successes—and maybe even stretch them a bit!

- Do's and don'ts. What presenters are most successful with this group and why? What have they seen too much of? Not enough of?

- Tolerance. What kind of interaction works best with this group?

- Risk. Does this audience prefer the tried and true or the original and unexpected? What can you do to be original, proactive, engaging, and involving?

- Terminology. What words, expressions, or phrases should you avoid? What are the group's preferred terms or acronyms that they use all of the time? For example, do they call a customer a client? A member? A user?

HOT BUTTONS. Are there any sensitive issues or current events you should be aware of?

ENERGY. Depending on when you will speak in the course of the day's program, you may need to bring more energy to your presentation.

- Program flow. What time of day will you be presenting? What happens before as well as after your presentation?

- Food. Will any food, beverages, or alcohol be served before or during the presentation?

AUDIENCE ALIGNMENT. You want to approach your topic from the *audience's* perspective, not your perspective.

- Outcomes. What are the expectations and desired outcomes as a result of your speech? What is the tone or feeling the participants should have at the end?

- Theme. Is there a theme or tagline associated with the presentation or conference?

- Expectations. What are the audience's expectations about this program, either from a historical point of view or the current buzz?

- Attitude. What is the general attitude or feeling toward the topic?

- What do you want people to be saying as they leave the room?

AUDIENCE CHARACTERISTICS. When you understand the personality of the audience, you can select just the right technique that engages rather than bores them.

INFUSE YOUR PRESENTATION

- Expertise. What is their knowledge level about this topic? Are they predominantly generalists or specialists? What are their key interests and concerns? What are their occupations, experience, and education levels?
- Bias. Is there a personal or professional bias toward your topic?
- Demographics. What is the gender and age mix? Is the group multicultural and/or international?
- Size. How many people will be in the audience? Is it an intimate group where everyone knows each other or a vast room chock-full of strangers?
- Formality. How formal will the presentation be? Will the audience be wearing business casual or formal attire?
- Disabilities. Do any of the participants have any disabilities you need to be aware of?
- Commonalities. What do you have in common with the group you'll be addressing? What hopes, dreams, and fears do you share? Are you similar in outlook, age, and experience? How are you different from them?

VENUE. Sometimes, the room logistics or site prohibits some types of interaction. Know these limitations up front in your planning so you don't have to adjust on the fly later.

- Seating. What is the planned seating and table configuration? Can it be changed?
- Lighting. Will the house lights be on or is there a spotlight at the front? You want to make sure the audience can see you wherever you may roam.
- Platform. Will there be a platform? How high will it be? Will there be stairs so you can move into the audience easily?
- Audiovisuals. Will you be using any AV aids? Where will the screen be placed? Will you be using a cordless microphone?
- Time. How much time has been allotted for this speech? Worst-case scenario: how much time might you end up with?

The more you know about the people in front of you, the better you will be able to connect with them. Each of these questions also has implications for which techniques you will select in order to engage and involve your audience.

EASY WAYS TO INVESTIGATE YOUR AUDIENCE

You may be saying to yourself, "Gosh, that's a lot of research I have to do!" Yes, it takes a bit of effort, but you will be rewarded handsomely for what you discover!

Here are resources to draw upon as you research and prepare your presentation:

MEETING PLANNER. Your first call should be to the person who asked you to give this presentation. This individual is usually the most reliable resource and can steer you toward these others who can also provide insights:

♦ Heavy hitters. Talk with the key influencers in the audience. For example, talk to the highest-ranking company officer, the most-respected technical expert, and the manager with the most authority to make decisions.

♦ Participants. Interview a few selected participants prior to your presentation or talk to them right before your speech as they wander into the presentation room.

INTERNET. Explore the company website and Google news, trends, media, and stories related to the topic, company, and industry.

PROMOTIONAL MATERIALS. Make sure you get copies of what has been sent to the participants and other promotions about the speech.

PUBLICATIONS. Acquire a copy of the organization's recent publications, newsletter, strategic plan (including mission, vision, values, and strategic goals), and any other documentation that might help you get a firm grasp of the issues the audience is facing.

STEP 2. LAY OUT YOUR PRESENTATION IN BITS

Right now, your speech may consist of a mental or written outline of key words and a slide show with or without notes. Or, you may even have it written out in text format. Don't worry; the process of dividing it into bits will work regardless of your preparation preference.

If you have an outline, put each point on an index card or sticky note. If you have a slide show, print out each slide with notes. If you have the text written out, cut each section into a bit of material.

INFUSE YOUR PRESENTATION

What is a bit? you may ask. My definition of a bit is a piece or segment in your speech that can be cut and pasted into another place within your speech. It is, in essence, one of the mini-conversations you have with your audience. It may be a sentence, a paragraph, a story, or an activity. Bits are usually in one-, two-, or three-minute chunks. Much like hanging ornaments on a Christmas tree, you hang these bits of material on the basic structure of your speech:

Open

Point 1

Point 2

Point 3

Close

1	Topic		Audience	
2	**Bit**			
3	Objective: • Know? • Do? • Feel?			
4	Current technique(s)	6	Possible technique	
5	Place on energy curve	7	Circle selected technique(s)	

If you have neither written nor prepared your speech, now would be a good time to create the outline. Outlines automatically segment your speech into bits because the key words you write down are a trigger to a specific bit in your mind.

STEP 3. IDENTIFY YOUR OBJECTIVE(S) FOR EACH BIT

Here's the tedious part. On each index card, write down the objective of each bit. Consider the objectives from a content perspective as well as according to their emotional connotation:

• What do you want the people to think?

• What do you want the people to feel?

• What do people need to know?

You might even have two objectives, so write the most important objective first and then the next. For example, is your objective for a particular bit in your presentation to

- Set the tone for interaction?
- Open the program?
- Capture the group's attention?
- Arouse participants' curiosity?
- Surprise the audience?
- Get personal/less formal?
- Collect information about the audience and their knowledge level?
- Elicit an emotional response?
- Introduce a concept?
- Understand or demonstrate a skill?
- Reinforce content?
- Inform the audience?
- Inspire the group?
- Energize the crowd (especially between 1:00 and 3:00 p.m.)?
- Create an action plan/inspire application?
- Close the program?
- Other?

You may be thinking, "Do I have to do this for every single bit?" Yes, you should, but you don't have to. This step is a key differentiator between merely peppering and thoroughly infusing your presentation. The technique(s) you select will reinforce each of the objectives, providing a smooth experience for your audience.

Let me give you an example of how important this step is. One of my clients, Judy, routinely gives a speech about surviving a workplace reduction in force, otherwise known as a layoff. She was looking for a new opening activity and told me about the types of activities she had been using. When I asked what the objective of the opening activity was, she said she wanted to shock the audience into the possibility that they too could be laid off. Well, not a single one of the activities she had been using was shocking! In fact, they were all quite pleasant—primarily because Judy is a genuinely nice lady. After we went through this process, she developed an amazing opening activity that grabs everyone's attention—even those who believe they will never be laid off.

You are naturally going to gravitate toward the techniques that are most comfortable for you unless you identify the objective first.

STEP 4. NOTE THE CURRENT TECHNIQUES

On each index card, note the presentation techniques you are currently using (or intend to use) in your speech. You can either write out the technique or you develop your own icons as a form of shorthand:

:-) = Smile

// = Pause

B = Breathe

ALL CAPS = Words you want to emphasize

(eye) = Look at the audience

< = Speak louder

> = Speak in a quieter voice (but one that's still audible)

SL = Move stage left

SR = Move stage right

§ = Tell a story

See? You are already using lots of engaging and interactive techniques! Most of them reinforce your stated objective, but a few of them might not. If they don't support your objective, then you may want to reconsider that technique.

STEP 5. LAY OUT THE ENERGY CURVES

Once you have your outline and current techniques, you will place your cards along an "energy curve," which will tell you whether you have enough energy flowing through your presentation.

To determine your energy curves, find out how much time you are expected to talk. Divide this time into equal segments—typically from six to eight minutes long (the duration of TV show segments between commercial breaks). The time length of each curve may be shorter, but no longer than eight minutes, depending on the total length of the speech, the number of points you have, the audience's personality, the time of day, and the food intake prior to your presentation.

Take several pieces of large paper (legal size, tabloid, or chart paper) and lay them out in a long line. Have one sheet of paper for each segment of your presentation. For example, if you've been asked to speak for thirty minutes you would have four to six pieces of paper spread out in a line on your desk or along the wall. I prefer to use an easel chart because it gives me more room to move things around. I also like to add a sheet of paper at the front titled "Set the Tone" and one at the end titled "Make It Stick" to capture the things I need to remember at the front end as well as after the presentation.

On each sheet of paper, draw half of a sine wave curve with the highest peak on the upper left side of the paper and the bottom of the wave on the lower right side of the paper.

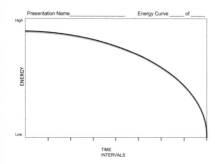 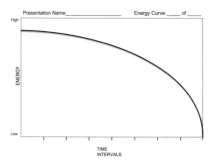

Now, place your bits in the program along the energy curves. Is the technique matching the energy curve pretty well? Relative to your other activities, are you moving from a high-energy, high-impact, and high-intensity technique to a less-intense activity?

More important, does the flow make sense to you? You don't have to force your material to fit these energy curves. They are only there as guidelines to help you make smarter choices.

INFUSE YOUR PRESENTATION

STEP 6. BRAINSTORM DIFFERENT TECHNIQUES

There are so many different possibilities to engage and involve the audience; it is truly limited only by your imagination. For each bit that needs a little boost of energy, brainstorm different techniques to reinforce its objective(s). Here are some ideas to help you get started:

SMALL STUFF. Think thirty-second bits or one-, two-, or three-minute bits rather than a colossal forty-five-minute activity.

EXPERIMENT. Think about the connections and associations the audience will be familiar with. Go through the list of techniques and just try it out. You might be surprised at what sticks!

PILLAGE YOUR PILE. You have been clipping short stories from magazines, newspapers, journals, and advertisements, as well as collecting interesting or startling facts, quotations, cartoons, and statements. Look through the pile of stuff you have accumulated and see how a few might be integrated into your presentation. (Note: Your pile of twenty tidbits typically will yield only a few that can be reasonably used at any given time!)

COMBINE. Take a few different techniques and see how they can be combined and used together or right behind each other.

GET INSPIRED. Watch the world around you and always be on the hunt for ways to engage your audience. You will find ideas where you least expect them; however, you must pay attention! (See chapter 15 for more ideas on where to get inspired.)

ASK YOUR FRIENDS. If you don't consider yourself to be very creative, take the point in your speech that you want to create an activity about and ask your friends what they would do.

STEP 7. SELECT THE MOST APPROPRIATE TECHNIQUE

For each bit, you now have a host of possible techniques to insert into your program. From the list of possibilities, select the most appropriate technique to fulfill the objective and keep the energy and the conversation flowing for that particular audience. Screen the list of techniques you've chosen through this filter:

ALIGNMENT. It is absolutely critical that your selected technique is aligned with the objective(s) for each of your bits and also with the overall meeting objectives or theme. Never lose sight of these two imperatives. Choose techniques that reinforce your presentation points. Nothing is more useless than activities with little connection to the purpose of your presentation.

RISK. Unless the audience already trusts you, move from low-risk techniques to higher-risk interactions.

PACE. Keep the energy up by changing the pace every six to eight minutes (the equivalent of one energy segment).

VARIETY. Do something different within each energy segment. Place the most energizing part of the activity at the front end of the segment. Audiences get bored easily with the same technique repeated ad nauseam.

SIZE. Some techniques are more effective with smaller groups; some are more appropriate for larger groups; still others can be used regardless of group size.

CHARACTERISTICS. Audiences are made up of people from many different cultures, backgrounds, and education levels. These characteristics all play a part in determining which techniques you should and should not select. Choose techniques that help bridge the gap between you and the audience by bringing out what you have in common.

ROOM SETUP. Depending on the venue, sometimes the room setup can be very restrictive. For example, if you are presenting in a confined space, you will have to modify an activity that requires a great deal of movement or select a different activity altogether.

TIME. Some techniques require no extra time at all, whereas others need a little additional time. Therefore, decide how you are going to incorporate techniques without sacrificing content.

BACKUP. When it comes to presentations, Murphy's Law reigns supreme: whatever can go wrong will go wrong. Have a backup plan B just in case your selected technique doesn't engage as well as you thought it would; there are more or fewer people than you expected; the room setup is different; or the nightmare for all interactive presenters—no one participates!

INFUSE YOUR PRESENTATION

PLAN B

If you are not connecting, smoothly downshift into plan B, that is, your backup plan for when things don't go according to plan. To create a solid backup plan, ask yourself, "What could go wrong during this presentation?" and then think about what you would do to turn that situation around. For example:

♦ The audience looks bored or restless. You could use more concrete examples or ask the audience to share an example. Change your location in the room by walking around the lectern or sitting on a desk. Cut it short by eliminating the subpoints.

♦ The participants are scribbling furiously. Slow down, pause, or let them know there will be a handout or takeaway at the end.

♦ The participants have puzzled looks. Acknowledge the looks and attempt to clarify your points.

  ♦ Say it differently—"In other words . . ."
  ♦ Explain your terms—"What that means is . . ."
  ♦ Add depth—"Another way to look at this is . . ."
  ♦ Define your acronyms—"That stands for . . ."
  ♦ Give an example—"For instance, there is the case for . . ."
  ♦ Provide evidence—"Research shows that . . ."

Finally, I always keep one or two provocative questions in my back pocket. You are guaranteed to get a conversation going with a well-phrased question.

STEP 8. DO A DRY RUN

You have mapped out your speech and feel confident that you have selected stellar techniques to engage and involve the audience. You have a crystal clear mental picture of what you must say and do to converse with the participants. You think you are ready, but you are not as ready as you should be. Remember Murphy's Law—especially when it comes to engaging and interacting with the audience. It makes perfect sense to practice those techniques that are new to you, along with any equipment that uses advanced technology.

ALONE. Initially, practice by yourself. Simulate as realistic an environment as you can. Stand up. Put some chairs in front of you. Get a feel for the flow and pace.

SMALL GROUP. Once you feel comfortable with the opening and closing bits as well as your new stuff, practice before a small group. Family, friends, and coworkers make great small groups. Practicing in front of a live audience increases your confidence in the material and your ability to adapt it to meet the needs of the participants.

ON LOCATION. If possible, practice in the actual room in which you will be delivering the presentation. This might be done the night before or the first thing in the morning of the presentation, when no one else is around. If you have merely a few minutes, practice the bits where you actually move into the audience or work with an audience member on stage.

Q&A. If you are going to have a Q&A session (see chapter 7) include the Q&A in your rehearsal:

- Develop a list of potential questions and suitable answers.
- Simulate the upcoming session by having a colleague ask some potential questions.

CRITIQUE. Videotape—or at the very least, make an audiotape of—your practice session and review it. Do not watch it more than once, however, lest you reinforce the not-so-good, the bad, and the ugly parts of your presentation.

CHECKLIST. As you practice your presentation, develop a checklist of all the stuff you need to bring, such as props, index cards, handouts, takeaways, A/V equipment, and the like (see chapter 2).

Keep improving your presentation with each practice run until you are ready for prime time!

  Don't forget to check out more resources and downloads at www.boringtobravo.com.

INFUSE YOUR PRESENTATION

CHAPTER FIFTEEN RECAP

In order to infuse your presentation with engaging and interactive techniques, follow this process flow:

Homework
1

Lay Out in Bits
2

ID Objectives
3

Note Techniques
4

Lay Out Curves
5

Brainstorm
6

Select Technique
7

Do a Dry Run
8

1. Do your homework about the audience

2. Lay out your presentation in bits

3. Identify your objective(s) for each bit

4. Note the current techniques

5. Lay out the energy curves

6. Brainstorm different techniques

7. Select the most appropriate technique

8. Do a dry run

ACTION PLAN

Based on the information in this chapter, I intend to

Continue _____

Start _____

Stop _____

CHAPTER SIXTEEN

IMPROVE YOUR PRESENTATION SKILLS

YOU'VE INVESTED BOTH your time and your energy in order to make your presentations more engaging and interactive. As a result of your efforts, you delivered a more engaging and interactive speech and, not surprisingly, people clapped at the end. As people were leaving, you could hear some memorable phrases being repeated here and there. Audience members responded enthusiastically to your follow-up e-mail. Life is good and all is well with the world.

Later on, you could be asked to give that same presentation elsewhere. You may be asked to give a modified version of that speech to a similar, yet different audience. You could pick out elements from this presentation to plug into a different presentation. Or, someone else may want to borrow your presentation to give to another group. Just because you delivered one presentation, it doesn't mean you are officially done with it.

If you are serious about improving your presentation skills, you should routinely critique yourself, collect audience feedback, and continue to invest in your professional and personal development.

CRITIQUE YOURSELF ⚠

The main way to learn how to better engage and involve your audiences is to present more frequently. Note what works and what doesn't work. Keep doing what works well and change the things that don't work as well. I realize how basic this sounds, but I am continually surprised at how seldom this happens.

You give the speech and then dash off to the next assignment. While you are driving, you think about what worked well and what you would do next time. And you *think* you will remember your observations. But you don't give another presentation for another few weeks, and when it rolls around, you have forgotten all the things you wanted to do differently the next time.

If you really want to improve your presentation skills, go the extra mile and critique yourself, using the self-assessment form on page 230. 🔍

The presentation self-assessment is a simple form to complete as soon as possible after you've delivered your presentation. It should take no more than thirty minutes to complete; then place it in a "continuous improvement binder." Periodically, you can flip through the binder to see themes, patterns, and trends as well as specific improvements for that particular speech—just in case you ever have to give it again.

1. Reflect. As soon as possible after your presentation, take a moment to reflect on what went well and what did not go so well.

2. Analysis. Ask yourself these two questions: "Why did that technique work?" "Why didn't that activity work as well as I thought it would?" Your answers could be a host of causes ranging from technique selection and your comfort level to the actual content and the audience's personality.

3. Upgrades. How would you improve the presentation the next time? Write down specifics about how you would change it. Even if you *never* give this speech again, still go through this process, as you may give a variation sometime later.

4. One Thing. Close to the bottom, draw a red line across the page. Write down the one thing you learned through this critique process. It could be something you want to reinforce or change for the next time.

IMPROVEMENT

5. Rate Yourself. Give yourself a realistic "grade" on a scale of 1 to 5 (with 1 being the lowest and 5 being the highest) for the overall presentation as well as each category technique. Any grade below a 5 is an opportunity for improvement.

6. Correlate Scores. As you tally the scores, note the areas for which only a "1" or a "2" was reported. Reflect on the comments made in the second open-ended question: "What would you do differently?" Is there a correlation? Note also the areas for which a "5" or a "4" was reported. Reflect on the comments made in the first open-ended question: "What worked well?" Is there a correlation?

7. Interpret Scores. Tally the scores in each category: Preparation, presence, and technique. For each category, if you scored between:

0–30   You are most likely new to presenting and this is one of the areas you need the most development in.

31–60   You have minimal to average ability in this area. Your limited skills will affect future presentations.

61–90   You are well on your way to having the skills required in this particular area. Note any specific items for which you rated lower. These are the skills you will most likely want to improve in future presentations.

91–120 You have developed excellent skills in these areas. Any questions that you answered with a "2" or less should give you pause to think about what you can do to improve that particular skill.

Do these scores match your overall presentation score? Do they align with the comments you made earlier?

8. Binder. Keep your self-evaluations in a binder. As you prepare for your next speech, flip through your binder and notice the trends in your comments, the one thing you learned through the self-evaluation process, and your assessment results. Notice the themes and trends that emerge.

9. Think Progress. You may not get a "5" in all categories to start, but you will see the results of the good work you do—and where you will still need to improve and progress over time.

SELF-ASSESSMENT FORM ⚠ ⚠

Instructions: As soon as possible after your presentation, complete this assessment form.

Presenter:_____

Presentation:_____

Audience:_____

Audience Size:_____

Date:_____

Duration:_____

What worked well and why?

What would you do differently and why?

What was said to you after your presentation?

Next Steps/Upgrades?

The One Thing I Would Do:

Use the following scale to rate your performance during this presentation:

1 – very poor

2 – poor

3 – average or not applicable

4 – very good

5 – excellent

Preparation

1. _____ Researched and analyzed the audience's expectations

2. _____ Was knowledgeable about the content of the presentation

3. _____ Integrated the meeting theme into the presentation

4. _____ Created and followed a solid structure or outline

5. _____ Created a "twitterable" headline or anchor for the main idea or body points

6. _____ Created a lively, interesting title

7. _____ Created intriguing preview or promotional material

8. _____ Designed and created visual aids and props that supported the presentation

9. _____ Prepared a handout or takeaway to complement the presentation

10. _____ Established a connection with the audience prior to the event

11. _____ Personalized the presentation with up-to-the moment "news" of the day

12. _____ Arranged and managed an inviting and engaging environment

13. _____ Had all supplies and equipment checked out, ready to go and operating appropriately

14. _____ Practiced and rehearsed the presentation

15. _____ Was ready for Murphy's Law: What could go wrong did—and I recovered magnificently!

Total _____

Presence

1. _____ Built credibility and rapport with the audience

2. _____ Showed passion about the topic

3. _____ Was genuine, transparent, and honest with the audience

4. _____ Was present (in the moment) with the audience

5. _____ Read/listened to the audience and gauged their response

6. _____ Appeared comfortable and relaxed

7. _____ Used my natural sense of humor effectively

8. _____ Smiled with the audience

9. _____ Dressed appropriately for the event

10. _____ Used vocal variety to emphasize key points

11. _____ Refrained from poor speaking habits (e.g., vocalized hiccups)

12. _____ Moved with a purpose

13. _____ Used inviting gestures

14. _____ Used silence/pause effectively

15. _____ Managed time effectively and ended on time

Total _____

Techniques

1. _____ Established a connection right before the start of the presentation

2. _____ Personalized the message to the audience

3. _____ Used inclusive language—more "we" than "me"

4. _____ Elected an appropriate and captivating opening

5. _____ Asked engaging questions effectively

6. _____ Told effective examples, interesting stories, and/or memorable metaphors

7. _____ Used audiovisuals smoothly and appropriately

8. _____ Effectively managed the audience's questions and answers

9. _____ Pre-empted their objections to participation

10. _____ Recognized and rewarded audience participation

11. _____ Used technology to engage the audience

12. _____ Involved the audience in a specific task, demonstration, or small group activity

13. _____ Interviewed an audience member effectively

14. _____ Finished with a strong call to action

15. _____ Created a structure for the audience to follow up or extend the conversation

Total _____

_____ + _____ + _____ = _____

Preparation + Presence + Techniques = Final Score

COLLECT AUDIENCE FEEDBACK ⚠

Once you finish your speech, ask for and listen to feedback from the audience. Yes, you want to make sure they were engaged, but you also want to know if the audience is walking away with something of value to them.

ACCEPT THE APPLAUSE. One way in which audiences tell you that they appreciated your presentation is through their applause. Be gracious and accept the compliment. Smile back at the audience to say "thank you."

BE AVAILABLE. Let people come up to you to share what's on their mind. This is good news; they want to continue the conversation in a more informal way with you. They might share a story or a different perspective, or they might just want to say thank you for coming.

LOOK AROUND. Are other audience members still milling about, talking to each other? They are still engaged and talking about the presentation. If they disperse too quickly, it might be that there is another meeting they need to attend or that there is simply nothing left to say.

LISTEN. It sounds rather creepy, but walk around and listen to the conversations. What are people talking about? Sometimes, the best feedback comes from lingering after your presentation or overhearing conversations in the restroom.

SEEK OUT OTHERS. You can also approach a few random audience members and ask what they are going to do as a result of your presentation. You can ask what they thought of your presentation. Were they engaged? What was the most memorable moment? What is their call to action?

SURVEY. For more formal presentations, you can hand out a short survey or send out a Web-based survey to get their reactions. I use the form in the following box to get audience feedback about my presentations.

PRESENTATION FEEDBACK FORM

This evaluation is designed to measure your satisfaction with the presentation you have just experienced, as well as to provide us with information to continually improve our seminars.

What was the most valuable idea you learned today and will use?

What did you want to receive but didn't?

How will your organization benefit from this experience?

On a scale of 1–5, rate the following (please circle):

	low				high
Overall	1	2	3	4	5
Content	1	2	3	4	5
Speaker quality	1	2	3	4	5
Knowledge of material	1	2	3	4	5
Handouts/visual aids	1	2	3	4	5

Additional Comments or Feedback:

Should we have Kristin back? ☐ Yes   ☐ No

If yes, which topics would you like her to speak on?

Thank you for helping us to improve our programs.

May we quote you? ☐ Yes   ☐ No

Please supply the following information to receive a free "The Extraordinary Team" newsletter.

Name _____

Organization _____

Address _____

City/State _____ ZIP Code _____

E-mail _____

Telephone ( ) _____

Fax ( ) _____

IMPROVEMENT

AUDIO/VIDEO CRITIQUE ⚠ ⚠ ⚠

Your self-assessment is invaluable. By documenting what worked well and what you would have done differently, you'll be able to upgrade your next speech, and the one after that, and the one after that—each and every time. That's how you will get better.

For the overachievers reading this book, would you like to get better even faster? You can accelerate your learning curve by recording your speech. The technologies for audio and audio/video capture are extremely accessible and affordable these days, so there is no reason why you can't. Just set up a small digital voice recorder or camera, turn it on, and give your presentation. 🔎 If it will

make you feel more comfortable, have a friend tape you. Don't worry about the digital quality; you're just making this for your own educational benefit—not to post on YouTube.com!

LISTEN TO YOURSELF. Use a tiny digital voice recorder that can download straight into your laptop. Using speech recognition software 🔎, you can easily make a transcript of your presentation from the recording. Go over the actual speech you gave (not the one you think you gave) and notice the language you use. Is it inclusive? Is it descriptive? Could you tell your stories a bit better? Make your small group activity directions clearer? Make notations on your transcript as you listen.

WATCH YOURSELF. If you have never watched a video of yourself, this may be a little unsettling, but you'll get used to it after you have watched yourself a few times.

1. The first time you watch the video, watch it by yourself with no other objective than to watch yourself. Get the curiosity out of the way.

2. The second viewing should be a thorough critique. Note what worked well and what didn't. It's easy to get caught up in all the "bad things"

you did. Don't. Give equal weight to the "went wells" and the "do differentlies." Think about the different techniques you used to engage the audience. If you have a transcript, note the significant bits that can be improved. Make comments on the side.

3. The third viewing should be with the volume turned all the way down. Note how you are nonverbally engaging the audience.

4. Finally, watch the video through the audience's eyes. In this case, invite a few friends to watch the video with you (but sit behind them so you don't influence their responses). Note when they become engaged and when they do not. Better yet, videotape the audience rather than (or in addition to) yourself—you'll be able to gauge the audience's level of interest.

ANOTHER PERSPECTIVE. Though it is helpful to do a self-critique, it is extremely valuable to ask a knowledgeable source to give you objective feedback. The person who is helping you should be a good speaker and someone whose opinion you value. If you can afford it, hire a reputable speech coach who will give you suggestions on how to improve your presentation.

KEEP LEARNING ⚠

You must have decided to read this book for a reason, presumably to improve your presentation skills, specifically in the area of making your presentations more engaging and interactive. Your learning journey should not stop where this book ends, however. Here are but a few of the myriad ways you can improve your presentation skills:

PRACTICE. Take small bits of your presentation and try them out on your friends, family, and coworkers. Notice when they engage with you, and—perhaps more important—when they don't!

SPEAK MORE. Put yourself in a position to *have* to speak more. Examples include taking a leadership role in your professional association, management club, or personal interest group. When you speak more, you speak better. Look for opportunities to speak in public:

- Tell an interesting story at the next party you go to.
- Offer to give a presentation at a group meeting.

- Speak for your favorite community cause.
- Submit a proposal to deliver a presentation at a professional conference.
- Talk to your training department or local college about being a guest presenter.

When you offer to help someone else, you end up helping yourself.

WATCH OTHERS. Admire the skills, talent, and style of the charismatic orators of today—and of years past—either live or on the Internet. ✎ Watch and learn from *anyone* who gives a presentation. You will see some great speakers, some good speakers, and some not-so-good speakers, and you can learn from *all* of them what to do and what not to do. Just be true to your own unique style.

WATCH TELEVISION. Watch improv shows such as Bravo TV's *Whose Line Is It Anyway?* and *Inside the Actors Studio*, talk shows such as *Oprah* and *Dr. Oz*, and food demonstration shows such as the *Rachael Ray Show* and *Emeril Live!*

READ. Be a voracious reader. You can check out the recommended resources section in this book as well as on my website, www.BoringToBravo.com. ✎

COLLECT. Clip out short vignettes/stories from magazines, newspapers, journals, and advertisements. Start creating a folder of interesting or startling facts, quotations, cartoons, statements, and stories you think can be integrated into your presentation.

GO TO TRAINING. There are a number of excellent providers of presentation skills training. Note which specialty you want some support in (engaging, stories, humor, stage presence, or all of it) and research the available resources. Do your due diligence by getting and validating testimonials. ✎

JOIN UP. If you are a public speaker—which means anyone who gives presentations to other people—join your local Toastmasters club. If you are a professional speaker—which means someone who gets paid to give a speech—join the National Speakers Association of the United States. (For international organizations, check out the website of the Global Speakers Federation for the appropriate country association.)

 Don't forget to check out more resources and downloads at www.boringtobravo.com.

CHAPTER SIXTEEN RECAP

 Now let's put it all together! It's one thing to read a book; it's another thing entirely to apply what you have learned. Go through your notes and identify the top three to five things in each category that you firmly believe will make a difference in upgrading your presentations:

Continue? _____

Start? _____

Stop? _____

Put a tentative date to the right side of each item. It's okay. No one will know other than you and the book. If you don't make it by the due date, just write in a new date. Without due dates, this plan becomes a dream and will be consumed by the urgencies of your days.

Now write these due dates in your calendar. You can do it! I know you can! It will take only a few more minutes to write each item on your task list.

When one of these items pops up on your calendar or task list, only *you* get to make the choice as to whether you do it, delete it, or move it forward. My hope is that you stay committed to improving your skills and either do it or move it to a day where you can do it. Perhaps knowing I'm rooting for you is all the encouragement you need.

ACTION PLAN

Based on the information in this chapter, I intend to

Continue _____

Start _____

Stop _____

CONCLUSION

REMEMBER BILL, the curmudgeonly VP of manufacturing we talked about in the introduction? I coached Bill through several of the techniques in this book, and his next presentation was vastly different from the one that preceded it. What did he do differently?

- He shifted his mind-set to be more engaging.
- He stepped away from the lectern and moved closer to the audience.
- He prefaced his remarks by saying he had a speech written out but that he wanted to know what they (the audience) wanted to talk about.
- He suggested a process to start: He wanted to note their questions first and then address them in the order that made sense. He then got audience agreement to proceed with the process.
- He ditched the PowerPoint slides and captured their questions on the humble easel chart.
- He used people's first names and affirmed the underlying intent of their questions.
- He answered their questions and added some personal and historical examples.
- And the curmudgeon even smiled a few times!

Although Bill had the same thirty minutes, he covered the same amount of material while engaging the audience. This time, he aced the course evaluations and people were talking about his presentation for months.

And you can do the same thing that Bill did. Now that you have a process for infusing your presentations and a notebook full of ideas, I encourage you to go from boring to bravo during your next presentation. Try one or two low-risk techniques to get started. I would also advise you *not* to pack your presentation with every single technique in this book. That would be overkill!

Then, seek out opportunities to go from boring to bravo and transform an average presentation into something more engaging and interactive. Whether it is your own or one that you are watching, you can always learn by evaluating a presentation. You will learn what works best for you, what fits your style, and what works best for different kinds of audiences.

I wish you well in your journey to engage and interact with your audiences. And, if you want to share a tip or a technique or a reaction to something you learned by reading this book, I would be honored to hear from you. Join the conversation on my blog at www.BoringToBravo.com or send me an e-mail at Kristin@BoringToBravo.com.

GLOSSARY AND INDEX OF TERMS

Accountability. A structure that allows participants to hold each other answerable to their commitments. 206

Acronym. A word formed from the initial letters of a group of words; NSA, for example, is an acronym for the National Speakers Association. 116

Acrostic. A word formed from the first letter in each line, or series of lines, that spells a word or phrase when taken in order; for example, NEWS, from North, East, West, and South. 126

Active voice. A verb form in which the subject of the sentence acts or does something. 127

Adapt. To adjust or modify the technique in order to make it suitable to the audience and your presentation style. 141

Adopt. To choose or take a technique as one's own. 149

Alliteration. The repetition of the same sound (usually consonants) at the beginning of words or in accented syllables. 130

Allusion. A brief, indirect reference to a person, place, or event that all can identify. 145

Analogy. A comparison of two things that are alike in some ways and different in others. 144

Anchor. A word, a phrase, a sound bite, or a statement that captures the essence of your speech or reinforces your call to action. 125

Anecdote. A short interesting or amusing incident or event that is often autobiographical. 149

Aphorism. A short saying that embodies a general truth or astute observation. 141

Aside. A digression from the main flow of the speech. 52

Attribution. Crediting the original source of material used in a presentation. 72

Audience response system (ARS). A methodology that allows participants to select or dial in a response that is then tabulated and displayed for the presenter and/or audience to view. $\mathcal{O}$ 89

Autoresponder. A word, phrase, sentence, or gesture that the audience is prompted to respond with as a specific answer. 154

Back channel. The digital communications that occur during and after a live presentation. 101

Bar chart. A visual diagram with parallel bars of varying lengths used to illustrate comparative data. 71

Bit. A short section of material that is easy to memorize. Also called a "chunk." 217

Blog. Short for "Web log." A website that displays in chronological order the postings by one or more individuals and usually has links to comments on specific postings. 24, 110

Borrowed story. An anecdote or narrative taken from another source. 151

Brainstorming. A creative technique used to generate a list of items. 193

Cadence. The rhythmic flow and sequence of sounds or words in a sentence. 130

Callback. A reference to a word or phrase mentioned earlier in your presentation or earlier in the sequence of events leading to your presentation.

Cartoon. An illustrated sketch or drawing that is usually humorous. $\mathcal{O}$ 68

Case study. A report of an individual unit or group, usually emphasizing developmental issues and relationships with the environment. 143

Cliffhanger. A technique in which a bit of a story ends in suspense in order to interest the reader or viewer in the next bit to be told later in the presentation. 154

Climax. The arrangement of words, phrases, or clauses in a sequence of increasing impact, with the strongest element (the climax) at the end. 127

Clip art. Predrawn pictures and symbols that computer users can add to a document. $\mathcal{O}$ 68

Closed question. A question that requires a one-word answer, typically yes or no. 83

Competition. A contest for a prize or recognition. 163

Content. The substantive information or creative material in a presentation in contrast to its actual manner or style of presentation. 12

Costume. A style of dress, including accessories and hairdos, characteristic of a period, place, person, etc. 29, 54

Countdown timer. A device that indicates the backward counting in fixed time units from the initiation to completion. $\mathcal{O}$ 77

Courier. A messenger, usually traveling in haste, to deliver or receive information, packages, etc., to or from the presenter and the audience. 159

CPAE. Council of Peers Award for Excellence, Speakers Hall of Fame, is a lifetime award conferred by the U.S. National Speakers Association for excellence and professionalism in speaking; given to speakers who have been evaluated by their peers and judged to have mastered seven categories: material, style, experience, delivery, image, professionalism, and communication. 116

Critique. A detailed evaluation or review. 228, 235

CSP. Certified Speaking Professional designation conferred by the National Speakers Association and the Global Speakers Federation; it is earned by demonstrating competence in a combination of professional standards: platform skills, business management, education, and association. 116

Debate. A discussion in which the affirmative and negative sides of a question are advocated by opposing speakers. 169

Definition. A statement of the meaning or significance of a word, phrase, or idea. 141

Demonstration. An exhibition of the operation or use of a device, machine, process, product, or the like to or with the audience. 166

Door prize. A prize awarded at an event either by chance through a drawing or as a reward. 62

Downstage. The front half of the stage closest to the audience. 43

Dyad. A group of two; also known as a pair or couple. 171

Easel. A tripod or frame used to support chart pads or other visuals at an angle. 62

Easel chart. A set of large sheets of paper, hinged at the top so they can be flipped over, upon which information is captured in sequence. 62, 172

Engage. When you attract an audience member's interest and attention. 5, 38, 177

Exaggeration. Grossly magnifying features or information to expanding or diminishing proportions. 129

Example. A bit used to clarify or elaborate on your point. 142

Expert. A person who has special skill or knowledge in some particular field. 26

Facilitator. A person responsible for guiding the work of a group to achieve a desired outcome. 186

Fact. A statement that can be verified, either by referring to a third source or by direct observation. 147

Fact-checking. To check the accuracy and source of an anecdote, definition, quotation, or statistic. 147

Fill in the blank. A technique whereby the speaker allows the audience to complete the empty space or pause in the sentence. 154

Fishbowl. A technique whereby the activities of a few participants are open to the view or scrutiny of the rest of the audience. 167

Fluffy word. A word that has little or no intellectual weight, such as "very" or "really." 128

Follow-up. An action that serves to increase the effectiveness of your previous presentation. 26

Freewheel. A brainstorming term used to signify that the participants are free to call out their ideas spontaneously. 191

Game. A competitive activity involving skill, chance, or endurance on the part of two or more persons who play according to a set of rules. ✎ 161

Gesture. A movement or position of the head, hand, arm, or face that is expressive of an idea, opinion, or emotion. 48

Gift. Something given voluntarily without payment expected in return. 62

Global Speakers Federation. An international association of independent professional speaker organizations from around the world (www. GlobalSpeakersFederation.org). 238

Google. A trademark used for an Internet search engine. 2, 152

Guidebook. An extended handout designed to guide the work of the participant, typically used in training sessions; also known as a workbook. 33

Handout. Any promotional or educational material given to each audience member. 33

Headline. A heading used to encapsulate more detailed subject matter containing one or more words and lines. 133

Heavy hitter. Those people in your audience who are very visible, well-known, and respected. 24, 217

Helper. A member of the audience whom you have asked to do something very specific for you. 160

Highlight. To emphasize or call attention to an important point. 133

HoF. Speakers Hall of Fame is a lifetime award conferred by the Canadian Association of Professional Speakers for outstanding performance as a professional speaker and dedication to the professional speaking industry by educating others to excel. Members are selected by their peers in recognition of their contributions. 116

Homework. Assigned work to be done prior to the presentation; also known as prework. 161

Hot seat. A position in which one person is subjected to extreme stress or discomfort, usually with on-the-spot coaching by the presenter. 167

House lights. Overhead lights that illuminate the meeting room. 31, 78

Humor. A comic, absurd, or incongruous quality causing amusement. 111

Hyperlink. To make a hypertext link in an electronic document. 66

Icebreaker. An activity, usually conducted at the beginning of a presentation, to warm up the audience. 𝒫 41

Icon. A sign representing its subject by virtue of a resemblance or analogy to it. 66

Illustration. An example that extends explanation or corroboration. 143

IMAG. An acronym for image magnification whereby the material the presenter has chosen is projected onto a large screen so the entire audience can see it. 182

Inducement. Something given that helps bring about an action or a desired result; also known as an incentive. 62

Influencer. A member of the audience who may not be a formal leader but nonetheless influences others within the audience. 24, 217

In medias res. "In the midst of things"; without preamble; the narrative starts literally in the middle. 39, 154

Interaction. A reciprocal action between the speaker and the audience. 157

Interview. A meeting or conversation in which a writer or reporter asks questions of one or more persons from whom material is sought for a newspaper story, television broadcast, etc. 24, 91

Intonation. The rise and fall of the voice when speaking. 47

Introducer. A person who presents the speaker to the audience. 40

Introduction. A short, personal presentation to introduce the speaker to the audience. 40

Irony. The use of words to convey a meaning that is the opposite of its literal meaning, such as "how nice!" when it really wasn't nice at all. 115

Jargon. Language peculiar to a particular trade, profession, or group. 116

Joke. Something said or done to create laughter or cause amusement. 121

Keynote. A speech, typically an hour or less in duration, that conveys one central theme. Also a software application by Apple for creating presentation slide shows. 7

KISS. Keep it Simple, Silly! 58, 135

Lectern. A stand with a slanted top used to hold a book, speech, or notes at the proper height for a speaker to deliver his or her program. Sometimes incorrectly called a podium. 32, 51

List. A series of names or other items in a meaningful grouping or sequence. 133, 161

Magic. The art of producing illusions as entertainment. 167

Meeting planner. The person in charge of planning the logistical arrangements of a meeting, such as room setup, hotel arrangements, meals, travel, and other program details; also known as the coordinator or organizer. 188

Mental imagery. A choice of descriptive words that brings a visual scene to mind. 128

Metaphor. A figure of speech in which a word or phrase is applied to something it is not ordinarily associated with, suggesting a resemblance to each other. 59, 144

Mingle. To mix with or join in with others. 37

Model. A representation, generally in miniature, to show the construction or appearance of an object or concept. 60

Movie clip. An excerpt from a telecast or full-length motion picture; also known as a video snippet. 🔎 73

National Speakers Association. The premier professional society in the United States dedicated to advancing the art and value of those who speak professionally (www.nsaspeaker.org). 238

Objective. The end result that one's efforts or actions are intended to attain or accomplish. 188, 218

One-liner. A short piece of humor easily inserted into a presentation. 133

Open-ended questions. A question that requires more than one word to answer. 82

Organization charts. A diagram representing how departments or divisions in an organization are related to one another along lines of authority. 71

Parallel construction. Consistent, identical structural patterns that create balance within a phrase or sentence or among several sentences. 131

Paraphrase. A restatement or rewording of a comment, giving the meaning in a clearer form. 105

Parody. A humorous or satirical imitation of a person, event, song, or piece of literature. 116

Participant. One who participates, shares, or takes part in a presentation. 18, 25

Participation. The act of taking part, sharing, or being involved in a presentation. 182, 186

Passive voice. A verb form in which the subject of the sentence is acted upon (i.e., receives the action). 127

Pause. A temporary stop or rest by a speaker. 131

Personal story. An anecdote or narrative based on your personal experience. 149

Pie chart. A graphic representation of quantitative information by means of a circle divided into sectors, in which the relative sizes of the areas (or central angles) of the sectors correspond to the relative sizes or proportions of the quantities. 71

Platform. A raised flooring or other horizontal surface upon which a presenter customarily stands; also known as a riser, stage, podium, or dais. 31

Poll. A collection of opinions on a subject for the purpose of analysis. 86

PowerPoint. A Microsoft application for creating presentations, speeches, slides, and handouts. 65

Prework. Assigned work to be done prior to the presentation; also known as homework. 24

Prize. A reward for winning or accomplishing a specific result. 62

Process. A systematic series of actions. 18, 188

Prop. An object used or handled by a speaker in a presentation; also known as property. $\mathcal{O}$ 59

Proverb. A short, popular saying, usually of unknown and ancient origin, that expresses some commonplace truth or useful thought. $\mathcal{O}$ 141

Provocative question. A question that provokes, incites, stimulates, irritates, or otherwise evokes feelings in the audience. 84

Public proclamation. To make one's intentions known publicly or openly. 206

Puzzle. A toy or problem to be solved by ingenuity or patient effort. 163

Quad. Short for the term "quadruplet," a group of four. 175

Question and answer (Q&A). An exchange of questions and answers between the speaker and the audience. 99

Queue. A literal or figurative line of people waiting their turn to speak. 104

Quiz. An informal test or examination. 161

Quotation. A statement by someone who is usually an authority or expert in the subject. 𝒫 141

Rapport. A harmonious or sympathetic relationship with the audience. 44

Recap. Short for recapitulation, a brief review or summary. 95

Recorder. A person whose official duty is to record in writing what has been said. 159

Reflection. The ability to give careful, quiet, thoughtful consideration to something. 205

Reframe. To restate an idea in another way in the attempt to help the audience understand and connect better with the idea. 95

Rehearse. To practice for a presentation in private prior to a public presentation. 50

Repetition. Stating verbatim something that has already been said. 127

Response cards. Color-coded index cards that create a visual response to a question. 𝒫 87

Restatement. To say again in a slightly different way something that has already been said. 127

Review. To go over the main points again in order to summarize or to enable higher retention of the information. 203

Revisit. To allow the audience to review the information in order to summarize or enable higher retention of the information. 203

Reward. Something given or received in return for something of merit. 61

Rhetorical question. A question asked solely to produce an effect or to make an assertion and not to elicit a reply. 86

Rhythm. The arrangement of words, vocalization, and silence to create an emotional balance. 130, 178

Role. A function, position, or task given to a person. 48, 172

Role-playing. An audience-involvement exercise in which the audience members and/or the presenter interact while assuming the attitudes, actions, and/or discourse of others. 168

Round-robin. A brainstorming technique in which the presenter calls upon participants around the room and then collects their comments. 87, 192

Rule of Three. A rhythmic structure that involves grouping three items together. When using humor, the first two items are serious and the third unexpectedly switches the pattern. 127

Run chart. A graphical representation of data in sequence over time, showing the trend line that reveals a general pattern of change; also known as a trend chart. 71

Runner. A courier who is assigned the responsibility of carrying the microphone to wherever the participants are seated/standing. 159

Sarcasm. The use of words or statements that convey the opposite of their literal or intended meaning. 106

Satire. The use of irony, sarcasm, ridicule, or the like in order to expose, denounce, or deride vice, folly, etc. 115

Show-and-tell. An activity in which each participant produces an object of unusual interest and tells something about it. 166

Sidebar. A specific type of aside during which the presenter steps out of role to make a parenthetical comment or remark. 52

Signature story or prop. A story or prop that is credited to a particular person. This type of story should never be used without permission of the owner. 149

Silence. The absence of any sound or noise. 82, 106

Simile. A figure of speech in which two unlike things are explicitly compared. 144

Sing-along. An informal or unrehearsed singing of a song by a group of people, usually under the direction of the speaker. 154

Site. The location of the presentation; also known as venue. 216

Situational question. A question that elicits the participants' experiences in a similar situation. 84

Slide show. The file or the display of a series of slides through a projector. 38, 65

Slip. A brainstorming technique in which each item is written on a separate slip of paper, a sticky note, or an index card. 192

Stage. A raised platform or floor upon which the presenter stands and delivers a speech from. 52

Stage left. The part of the stage that is left of center as the presenter faces the audience. 40

Stage right. The part of the stage that is right of center as the presenter faces the audience. 40

Staging. To use different parts of the stage for different purposes within your presentation. 52

Statistic. A numerical fact or figure that typically shows the relationship between the part and the whole. 148

Stock photos. Digital photographs that are typically purchased for use in slide shows or promotional materials. 🔎 68

Story. A narrative, either true or fictitious, designed to interest, amuse, or instruct the listener. 139

Survey. A collection of facts, figures, or opinions taken and used in the preparation of a presentation. 🔎 24

Symbol. A word, phrase, or image that represents or stands for something else. 68

Takeaway. Printed material or other gift that is handed out after the presentation. 33, 208

Teaser. An advertisement that lures people to your presentation. 25

Testimonial. A declaration made by a respected expert or authority in support of a person's character, conduct, qualifications, or that speaks to the value or excellence of a thing. 141

Theme. A unifying or dominant idea within the presentation. 28

Timekeeper. A person who keeps time either to ensure that the presentation ends exactly on time or to announce the amount of time left. 159

Toastmasters. A nonprofit organization dedicated to helping people become more competent and comfortable speaking in front of an audience (www. toastmasters.com). 128, 238

Transcribe. To make a written copy of a presentation. 135, 235

Triad. A group of three. 171

Tweet. Text-based posts of up to 140 characters that are circulated through Twitter. 101

Twitter. A free social networking and microblogging service that enables its users to send and read messages known as "tweets." 101

Upstage. The rear half of the stage farthest from the audience. 53

Usher. A person who escorts people to seats. 159

Vanna. An allusion to Vanna White, the hostess on the popular game show *Wheel of Fortune*. 160

Venn diagram. A diagram that uses circles to represent groups of things and their relationships. 72

Venue. The location of the presentation; also known as site. 216

Video snippet. A small excerpt from a video; also known as a movie clip. 73

Visualization. A technique used to have the audience recall or create a mental image or to picture a specific situation. 153

Visual. Any item or element that depends on the viewer's sense of sight. 57

Vivid words. Descriptive words that paint a mental picture in the listener's mind. 128

Vocalized hiccup. A filler word that has no meaning, such as "well," "ah," "umm," or "you know." 18, 128

Volunteer. A person who volunteers for a service or an undertaking. 92

Whisper. Attention-gaining technique in which the presenter speaks with soft, hushed sounds to one audience member. 48

Wimpy word. A timid word or phrase that conveys that the speaker is uncertain, such as "perhaps," "sort of," or "it seems like." 128

Workbook. An extended handout designed to guide the work of the participant, typically used in training sessions; also known as a guidebook. 33

RECOMMENDED RESOURCES

HERE IS AN ALPHABETICAL LIST, grouped by category, of the best books on my bookshelves. For more up-to-date resources and hyperlinks to other websites, please go the recommended resource tab on my website, www. BoringToBravo.com.

BASIC PRESENTATION SKILLS

The Exceptional Presenter by Timothy J. Koegel, Greenleaf Book Group, 2007. A good, solid foundation in presentation basics.

How to Write and Give a Speech by Joan Detz, St. Martin's Griffin, 2002. Joan gives step-by-step instructions to create an effective presentation.

I Can See You Naked by Ron Hoff, Andrews & McMeel, 1992. An enjoyable read that covers the do's and don'ts in a humorous way.

Public Speaking for Success by Dale Carnegie and Arthur Pell, Penguin Books, 2005. This is the bible for public speaking.

Speaking Is an Audience-Centered Sport by Marjorie Brody, Career Skills Press, 1998. An excellent primer on speaking to audiences large and small.

ENGAGEMENT AND INTERACTION

Give Your Speech, Change the World by Nick Morgan, Harvard Business Press, 2005. In my opinion, one of the best books on having an engaging mind-set and being focused on the audience.

The Instant Trainer by C. Leslie Charles and Chris Clarke-Epstein, McGraw-Hill, 1997. Although they focus on the trainer, Leslie and Chris pack in lots of interactive ideas you should feel free to adapt for your presentations.

Wake 'Em Up Presentations by Tom Antion, Anchor Publishing, 1997. Great, humorous book full of ideas and examples.

MODELS

The Power of the 2x2 Matrix by Alex Lowy and Phil Hood, Jossey-Bass/Wiley, 2004. This volume explains more than fifty classic models for strategic, organizational, and personal decision making.

POWERPOINT

Presentation Zen by Garr Reynolds, New Riders Press, 2008. The best book on the market when it comes to using PowerPoint.

The Visual Slide Revolution by Dave Paradi, Communications Skills Press, 2000. Dave provides great insight on how to make a slide presentation more visual and interesting.

QUESTIONS

Brave Questions by Alan R. Zimmerman, Zimmerman Communi-Care Network, Inc., 2003. This book is chock-full of provocative questions to get the conversation past the superficial.

The Conversation Piece by Bret Nicholaus and Paul Lowrie, Ballantine Books, 1992. This book is also full of questions to get the conversation started.

Making Questions Work by Dorothy Strachan, Jossey-Bass/Wiley, 2006. One of the best books on using questions effectively.

75 Cage-Rattling Questions to Change the Way You Work by Dick Whitney and Melissa Giovagnoli, McGraw-Hill, 1997. One of my favorite books to shake up my thinking about asking a great, provocative question.

HUMOR

The Comedy Bible by Judy Carter, Fireside Book, 2001. Aptly named.

Don't Let the Funny Stuff Get Away by Jeanne Robertson, Rich Publishing, 1998. Not only is Jeanne one of the best humorists I have ever heard, she also shares freely her process for finding humor in the world around us.

The Light Touch: How to Use Humor for Business Success by Malcolm Kushner, Simon & Schuster, 1990. The best book on business humor I've ever read.

The New Comedy Writing Step by Step by Gene Perret, Sanger, 2007. Gene was Bob Hope's comedy writer and this is a true classic on writing humor.

Punchline Your Bottom Line: 76 Ways to Get Any Business Audience Laughing by David Glickman, Keynote Comedy, 2003. David sparks your creativity to be able to create your own humor.

STORIES/WORD CHOICE

Choosing Powerful Words by Ronald H. Carpenter, Allyn & Bacon, 1999. A deep dive into picking an eloquent string of words.

Eloquence in Public Speaking by Kenneth McFarland, Prentice-Hall, 1961. Written by one of the most eloquent professional speakers in the United States; you won't be able to put this book down.

The Leader's Guide to Storytelling by Stephen Denning, Jossey-Bass/Wiley, 2005. A must-read for anyone needing to tell a story within a corporate setting.

GAMES

There are dozens (if not hundreds) of books on icebreakers, warm-ups, team activities, games, etc., that may inspire you to try something different.

All of Ed Scannell's titles in the *Games Trainers Play* series, particularly *The Big Book of Team Building Games* and *The Big Book of Business Games*.

Jossey-Bass/Pfeiffer publishes lots of books on team-building activities, and I have contributed to several edited by Elaine Biech: *90 World-Class Activities by 90 World-Class Trainers*, 2007, and *The Pfeiffer Book of Successful Team-Building Tools*, 2001.

Team Energizers by Kristin Arnold, QPC Press, 2003. Fifty practical team activities that I have personally used during various facilitated sessions.

FACILITATION

Facilitating with Ease! by Ingrid Bens, Jossey-Bass, 2000. A basic primer on facilitation. All of Ingrid's work is full of practical tools and techniques.

Facilitator's Guide to Participatory Decision-Making by Sam Kaner, New Society Publishers, 1996. One of the founding fathers of facilitation, Sam has written a classic that is both visually appealing and highly useful.

The International Association of Facilitators' Handbook of Group Facilitation edited by Sandy Schuman, Jossey-Bass/Wiley, 2005. A compendium of different competencies, skills, tools, and techniques of seasoned, professional facilitators such as myself. Check out my chapter (28) on "How to Build Your Expertise in Facilitation."

The Skilled Facilitator by Roger Schwarz, Jossey-Bass, 1994. This is the bible of facilitation. It's a little academic and esoteric at times, but well worth the read.

Team Basics by Kristin Arnold, QPC Press, 1999. My very first book and, as the title implies, a basic book about how to be a great team.

ACKNOWLEDGMENTS

This book would not have been possible without the inspiration of my fellow professional speakers from around the world. I am honored to have chronicled the various techniques they use to engage, involve, and inspire their audiences. Specifically, I'd like to thank the following speakers who have graciously shared their wisdom not only with me over the years of working together, but with you, the reader.

If you get a chance, go to their website and check out their videos—you'll see some amazing talent and you might even get a few ideas!

Betsey Allen, MBA, CSP, CQM	www.GainingResults.com
Tom Antion	www.Antion.com
Brian Tracy, CPAE	www.BrianTracy.com
George Campbell, CSP, CPAE	www.joemalarkey.com Brad McRae
Bill Cates, CSP	www.ReferralCoach.com
Eric Chester, CSP, CPAE	www.GenerationWhy.com
Chris Clarke-Epstein, CSP	www.Change101.com
Roxanne Emmerich, CSP, CMC, CPAE	www.EmmerichGroup.com
Tim Gard, CSP, CPAE	www.TimGard.com
Kit Grant, CSP, HoF	www.KitGrant.com
Amanda Gore, CSP, CPAE	www.AmandaGore.com
Lou Heckler, CSP, CPAE	www.LouHeckler.com

Ann Herrmann Nehdi	www.hbdi.com
Sam Horn, CSP	www.SamHorn.com
Shep Hyken, CSP, CPAE	www.Hyken.com
Elizabeth Jeffries, CSP, CPAE	www.TweedJeffries.com
Frank Kelly	www.FrankKelly.net
Victoria Labalme	www.VictoriaLabalme.com
Michael Soon Lee, MBA, CSP	www.EthnoConnect.com
Mike McKinley, CSP, CPAE	www.RealMikeMcKinley.com
Brad McMillian, CA	www.mpiweb.org
Brad Montgomery, CSP	www.BradMontgomery.com
Sue Morter, PhD	www.DrSueMorter.com
Dave Paradi	www.ThinkOutsideTheSlide.com
Randy Pennington, CSP, CPAE	www.PenningtonGroup.com
Bob Pike, CSP, CPAE	www.BobPikeGroup.com
Vince Poscente, CSP, CPAE, HoF	www.VincePoscente.com
Dan Poynter, CSP	www.parapublishing.com
Steve Rizzo, PhB, CPAE	www.SteveRizzo.com
Mark Sanborn, CSP, CPAE	www.MarkSanborn.com
Ed Scannell, CMP, CSP	www.EdScannell.com
Joseph Sherren, CSP, HoF	www.Ethos.ca
Kim Snider	www.KimSnider.com
Steve Spangler, CSP	www.SteveSpangler.com
Thiagi	www.Thiagi.com
Jeff Tobe, CSP	www.JeffTobe.com
Brian Walter, CSP	www.ExtremeMeetings.com
Joel Weldon, CPAE	www.SuccessComesInCans.com

ABOUT THE AUTHOR

KRISTIN ARNOLD, MBA, CMC, CPF, CSP, is passionate about making all presentations and meetings more engaging, interactive, and collaborative. As a high-stakes meeting facilitator, trainer, and keynote speaker, Kristin has worked with thousands of senior executives, project managers, and team leaders in Canada and the United States, challenging their traditional notions about teamwork. Her talent is all-around process—knowing the best way to get from one point to another, while cementing commitment to the final result. She is known for her concrete approach to teamwork and a treasure trove of practical concepts, tools, and techniques her clients can apply immediately to see positive, substantive results. Kristin was one of the first female graduates of the United States Coast Guard Academy and the first woman stationed onboard the USCGC *Buttonwood*, a seagoing buoy tender. She parlayed her understanding of teams and teamwork with an MBA in marketing strategy into a specialized management consulting firm focused on building extraordinary teams in the workplace. Kristin is on the Executive Development Faculty in the Schulich School of Business at York University in Toronto. She divides her time between Scottsdale, Arizona, and Cape Traverse, Prince Edward Island Canada.

**CARDS MUST REMAIN IN THIS
POCKET AT ALL TIMES**
A charge will be made for
lost or damaged cards